Fifteen Faces of God

Fifteen Faces of God

*A Quest to Know God Through
the Parables of Jesus*

Michael Manning

DOUBLEDAY

New York London Toronto Sydney Auckland

ⅅⅅ

DOUBLEDAY

Copyright © 2010 by Michael Manning

All rights reserved.

Published in the United States by Doubleday Religion,
an imprint of the Crown Publishing Group,
a division of Random House, Inc., New York.
www.crownpublishing.com

DOUBLEDAY and the DD colophon are registered
trademarks of Random House, Inc.

Scripture texts in this work are taken from the *New American Bible with
Revised New Testament and Revised Psalms* © 1991, 1986, 1970 Confraternity
of Christian Doctrine, Washington, D.C., and are used by permission of the
copyright owner. All Rights Reserved. No part of the *New American Bible* may
be reproduced in any form without permission in writing from the
copyright owner.

Library of Congress Cataloging-in-Publication Data
Manning, Michael, 1940–
Fifteen faces of God : a quest to know God through the parables of
Jesus / Michael Manning.—1st ed.
p.   cm.
1. Jesus Christ—Parables. 2. God (Christianity)—Knowableness. I. Title.
BT375.3.M34 2010
226.8—dc22
2009033852

ISBN 978-0-385-53161-0

PRINTED IN THE UNITED STATES OF AMERICA

Design by Jennifer Ann Daddio/Bookmark Design & Media Inc.

1   3   5   7   9   10   8   6   4   2

First Edition

May Jesus' love for the Father be a
source of unity for all people of faith.

"Come," says my heart, "seek God's face"; your face,
LORD, do I seek!
Do not hide your face from me.
—PSALM 27:8–9

Contents

Author's Note   ix

Introduction   1

1. Searching   15
2. Humble   24
3. Listening   33
4. Giving   45
5. Celebrating   52
6. Loving   61
7. Poor   75
8. Forgiving   90
9. Authentic   106
10. Generous   118
11. Risking   127
12. Proud   138
13. Patient   149
14. Trusting   163
15. Optimistic   174

Conclusion   187
Parables   189
Acknowledgments   191

Author's Note

One of my earliest understandings of God was that his love was limited. Now I know this to be untrue. God loves everyone unconditionally, and he wants us to respect and care for all people regardless of their beliefs or faith. He wants us to be enriched by each other. He wants us to consider each other as brothers and sisters. I write this book with the hope that *all people* who are seeking God will delight in the insights into the Father that Jesus shares with us. Please join me as we reverently journey through the teachings of Christ to uncover fifteen faces of an immensely wonderful God.

Jesus calls God his Father, and for this reason I use the male pronoun for God. Although God is spirit, neither a man nor a woman, the parables show faces of God that are rich in male and female characteristics.

Fifteen Faces of God

Introduction

Dramatize the parables of Jesus. I enthusiastically jumped at the idea. The production team of our national TV program had made the suggestion and I dove right in. Little did I know at the time that it would be the beginning of a profound and unexpected spiritual journey to discovering God through the parables of Jesus.

I love stories. I am pleased that Jesus loved stories too. He liked them so much that the Gospel of Mark 4:34 tells us, "Without parables he did not speak to them"—*them* being his followers and the masses of people who sought out Jesus in the beginning of the first century.

As the producer and the writer for the proposed television programs, I prepared for the writing of the scripts by going back and studying in detail the parables of Jesus. To my amazement, these stories came alive in a totally new way. I had always known that the parables were Jesus' main tool for teaching, but I began to see a pattern in these lessons that for some reason had eluded me for years. What was that pattern, you may be asking? I'll get to that in a moment.

Scripture scholar C. H. Dodd defined a parable as a story "drawn from nature or common life, arresting the hearer by

its vividness or strangeness and leaving the mind in suf-
ficient doubt about its precise application, to tease it into
active thought" (C. H. Dodd, *The Parables of the Kingdom*
[New York: Charles Scribner], p. 428). Some parables are
similes and use the words *like* or *as* to explain their meaning:
"The Kingdom of heaven is like a mustard seed." Others use
metaphors to get their point across, as in "You are the light of
the world" (Matthew 5:14). But regardless of the technique
used, each parable pushes—and teases—the audience to
think and ask questions. What does this story mean? Why is
it important? How does this relate to my life?

These "teasers" were directed to the large groups of people who followed Jesus. He knew that if he was going to keep
their attention, his stories couldn't be all about holy people in
the Temple and synagogue. The stories needed to be about
common, everyday people. And Jesus was a good showman.
He knew that the crowds would respond to stories of corruption, humor, and violence. And he gave them what they
wanted. A steward cheats his master. A lowly widow over-
comes a powerful judge. And when a manservant abuses fellow servants while the master is away, the master returns and
cuts him up into little pieces. Luke 12:46. Move over *CSI*!

Many of the parables were allegories, and sometimes in
private Jesus would explain a tale's hidden significance to
his disciples. An allegory is a story in which the people and
things stand for abstract ideas. For instance, in the parable
of the sower, Jesus explains to his disciples that the seed is
meant to represent the *word of God*:

"The seed sown on the path is the one who hears the word of the kingdom without understanding it, and the evil one comes and steals away what was sown in his heart. The seed sown on rocky ground is the one who hears the word and receives it at once with joy. But he has no root and lasts only for a time. When some tribulation or persecution comes because of the word, he immediately falls away. The seed sown among thorns is the one who hears the word, but then worldly anxiety and the lure of riches choke the word and it bears no fruit. But the seed sown on rich soil is the one who hears the word and understands it, who indeed bears fruit and yields a hundred or sixty or thirtyfold."
(Matthew 13:19–23)

For Jesus, something is always pointing to something else, and that's what's so exciting about these stories. The parables are multidimensional, and each of them is always leading us to a new understanding of God the Father.

The TV Scripts

As I began writing the scripts on the parables, I saw these stories in new and beautiful ways. I did not tamper with the basic tale. Yet, with a little poetic license, I expanded some of the stories by creating names for the anonymous characters in the originals. I created back stories about their families, their fears, their failures, and their dreams. In many ways these scripts were an exercise in Ignatian spirituality. Saint Ignatius of Loyola (1491–1556) encouraged this expansion of the Scripture through the use of the imagination as a form of meditation that could be used to help bring us more intimately into relationship with God.

For example, one of our dramatizations would tell the story of the rich man and Lazarus from the Gospel of Luke. The rich man (in our version his name is Mali) is very concerned with growing his flower business. He had great success: He had an expensive chariot, great clothes, vacations on the beach, a wife, three children, and a mistress in town for when things got boring at home. His biggest problem was this guy Lazarus who kept hanging around his front door looking for a handout. He was a bother. Mali was convinced that he lost clients because of this unsightly man hanging around his front door. He would move the poor man along, but he kept coming back.

Then both men died. Lo and behold, Lazarus ends up in the lap of Abraham and Mali is burning in hell. The last is first, the first last.

In another episode we enter into the delightful circumstances of Rufus (again a created name for our show) who discovers a buried treasure. Years before when the Assyrian army had swept into Israel to take slaves, the former owner of the property had buried the family treasures of gold and silver. The hero of this parable was hired to dig a well, and as he did so his shovel hit the buried box of gold and silver. He removed some of the treasure, covered up his find, and calmly bought the property, knowing he had found something that would change his life forever.

These scripts, which developed over some months, were fun to write, and they really got under my skin. I could feel something germinating in me. When they were ready we put an ad in a Hollywood theatrical magazine for actors to play the people in the parables. We described some of the biblical characters. Unfortunately, we would not be able to pay anyone, but the dramas would air on our national TV network. The response was overwhelming. We received over a thousand responses. Certainly, since we are located near Los Angeles, finding an actor isn't too difficult a job, but I really felt that the spirit of God was moving through this project and that there was something about the topic that appealed to people in a very important way.

During the months of writing, rewriting, auditioning, rehearsals, and production, I found myself growing in my appreciation and understanding—of Jesus' parables. It was during this immersion, through hours of praying and reading, that one thing became very clear, something that I had known my whole life intellectually but now felt emotionally: Jesus' life and ministry were a means of calling people's attention to his Father.

Jesus Tells Us About His Father

The Gospels are filled with rich expression of the intimate and humble relationship that Jesus has with his Father:

- Jesus prayed to the Father in public. (Luke 10:21)
- Mark tells us he rose early in the morning to be with his Father in prayer. (Mark 1:36)
- When asked by his followers how to pray, Jesus didn't say to pray to him. We should direct our prayers to "Our Father." (Matthew 6:9)
- "I don't speak on my own. I say only what the Father who sent me has told me to say. I know his commands will bring eternal life. That is why I tell you exactly what the Father has told me." (John 12:49)
- "The words that I say to you I do not speak on my own; but the Father who dwells in me does his works. Believe me that I am in the Father and the Father is in me." (John 14:10–11)
- "I obey my Father, so that everyone in the world might know that I love him." (John 14:31)
- Speaking to his Father, Jesus says, "I have brought glory to you here on earth by doing everything you gave me to do." (John 17:4, 6, and 26)
- "You have given me some followers from this world, and I have shown them what you are like." (John 17:26)

Then as Jesus nears his death, the Bible speaks of his intense love for his Father and desire to do his will:

- In the garden Jesus pleads three times with the Father to let his pending cruel death pass. (Luke 22:42) The letter to the Hebrews says in that moment he "learned obedience" to the Father. (Hebrews 5:8)
- But then in his last breath he says, "Father, into your hands I commend my spirit." (Luke 23:46)

Given this love for his Father, and the strong use of parables in Jesus' teaching—"He spoke to them in parables only" (Matthew 13:34)—we can easily conclude that the parables are a rich showcase of Jesus' creative way to show us the faces of his Father.

For this reason I have written *Fifteen Faces of God*. Jesus' parables show us the many loving sides of God. These stories are the adoration of a son for his Father, and they show us who God is and how he relates to humanity and to the world, his beloved creation. Just as our faces act as the windows to our authentic selves, the parables provide glimpses of the glory of the Father. They let us meet God eye-to-eye, and we come to know his nature as a seeking, listening, celebrating, generous, and loving Father.

Why Faces of God?

Why speak of God's faces? How can God have a face? Everyone knows that God is a spirit and as such has no physical parts. God is not male or female. He's not tall or short, not thin or chubby. *God just Is*, and he tells us to stay away from making images that depict him. The Hebrews would not even speak God's name, and in the Old Testament God tells his people through Moses, "You shall not have other gods besides me. You shall not carve idols for yourselves in the shape of anything in the sky above or on the earth below or in the waters beneath the earth" (Exodus 20: 3–4). God does not want strange gods to take his place. He does not want an image that will restrict his greatness.

Still, our minds are such that we cannot help but conjure up images of someone when we hear about him or her. The human mind is a natural image maker, and timeless images run through the Bible. God talks with Moses from the burning bush. God wrestles with Jacob before he meets his brother, Esau. God comes in the form of an angel to Gideon. These are all manifestations of God the Father.

Moreover the Hebrew Bible speaks frequently of God's face:

> *The* LORD *used to speak to Moses face to face, as one man speaks to another.* (Exodus 33:11)

[The Lord gave Aaron a blessing to say over the people:]
The LORD bless you and keep you! The LORD let his
face shine upon you, and be gracious to you! (Numbers
6:25)

[Job] shall pray and God will favor him; he shall see
God's face with rejoicing. (Job 33:26)

And did you know that the Psalms refer to God's face twenty-five times! Here are just a few examples.

"Come," says my heart, "seek God's face"; your face,
LORD, do I seek! (Psalm 27:8) My being thirsts for God,
the living God. When can I go and see the face of God?
(Psalm 42:3)

Awake! Why do you sleep, O LORD? Rise up! Do not
reject us forever! Why do you hide your face; why forget
our pain and misery? (Psalm 44:24–25)

Reading these passages, it is undeniable that the Hebrews longed to see God's face, and this is exactly what Jesus revealed using his stories. Jesus is the fulfillment of all the promises that God made in the Old Testament, and part of the salvation that he brings is his unveiling of the Father's face. "When can I go to see the face of God?" the Psalm asks. The answer is now.

My Images of God

Writing the scripts for my television show and later writing this book pushed me to take a personal inventory of my images of God the Father, and the changes my understanding has undergone over the course of my life. I do not believe I am alone in this journey of faith. The faces of God I describe here are a compilation of many factors that included pieces of art and what others have told me.

As a child growing up in a Catholic household, my introduction to the images of God came through pictures drawn by other people. There was the throne, the white beard, and the flowing robes. God was awesome, distant, powerful, and fearsome. In these images God was a God of justice. He was a *judge*. He was concerned with laws. If you did not obey those laws, God was going to get you. These were somewhat terrifying images for a young child, and I was constantly reminded by priests and the religious in my life that hell was a vivid possibility if God found me wanting at the time of my death. This is not to say that every image scared the pants off me. I frequently heard of God's love, yet I still found myself concentrating more and more on a God of judgment, so much so that I became preoccupied with making sure I would not die on the wrong side of a judging God. There were so many laws: no meat on Fridays; go to Mass on Sundays; go to confession once a month; don't have impure thoughts. God wanted us to be perfect, but as imperfect creatures how could we hope to even come close?

To make matters worse, in grade school I started reading the Bible and my fear of God grew more and more. God was angry. He put Adam and Eve out of the garden. He destroyed Sodom. And without misgivings, he slaughtered hundreds of thousands of men, women, and children at the hands of Gideon, Saul, and David and their armies.

God's Acceptance of Me

While my early images of God were shaped by fear, there were still some loving and hopeful people who talked about God and love in the same sentence. This loving image of God became most concrete for me when I was a young man in my twenties. At that time, in the early 1960s, the Catholic Church was going through a radical reexamination of itself. A new pope, John XXIII, began the Second Vatican Council. Over two thousand bishops looked at the way the Church spoke to the world, how it worshipped, and how it could move people to a renewed love of the Bible. In the process there was a reinvigorated way of looking at God the Father, not as an angry God of condemnation, but as a loving parent who wanted the best for you and me. Over time I found an ongoing freedom, peace, friendship, and a burning love in my relationship with God.

Paradoxically, though I was a Catholic, it was a Lutheran theologian, Paul Tillich, who wrote words that resonated deeply in my soul when I was in my midtwenties. These sentences of inspiration encapsulated my new loving bond with God:

> You are accepted. You are accepted, accepted by that which is greater than you, and the name of which you do not know. Do not ask for the name now; perhaps you will find it later. Do not try to do anything now; perhaps later you will do much. Do not seek for anything; do not perform anything; do not intend anything. Simply accept the fact that you are accepted. (*The Shaking of Foundations*, p. 162)

These words overwhelmed me. This sense of acceptance blurred the fearful images of God I had built up. Even though he might be a judge, God was now a compassionate judge. Even though he could be an angry God, that anger was coupled with empathy. And even though I didn't have a convincing answer to why God the Father of all creation permitted so many tragedies in the lives of human beings (murder, war, cancer, natural disasters), I began to grow, thanks to his acceptance of me, which provided me security in the midst of life's absurdities and injustices.

At the center of this new understanding was God's only Son. Jesus helped me include love in my image of God. In an overwhelmingly intimate favor, God sent his Son to become a human being, and in this Son I am able to see the face of God and actually love him as a friend and a brother.

Even though I am a priest and have been for over thirty years, I am still growing in my understanding of the love of God for me. The parables have brought me to a new level of insight, and many of those nagging, fearsome ideas of God have been replaced with fresh, grace-filled images. The parables of Jesus reveal a God of passion who is forgiving, patient, caring, and empowering. He assists us when we're broken and forgotten. He is perturbed when we're being hypocrites. He loves in a way that grates against our sense of justice. He is exciting and ready for a celebration. He delights in conversation. He listens. And after he hears our side, he's open to change his opinion. He loves every person he has created regardless of denomination and religion.

This book is a series of reflections and meditations on the love God has for all of his creation. The fifteen parables I have chosen spoke most clearly to me of Jesus' desire to tell us of his Father. And though this book is not meant to be an exhaustive study of parables, I do hope that our short journey together will bring you closer to Jesus' Father, who is undoubtedly our Father too. Come, let's discover some of God's faces and accept the challenge to mirror these faces to the people of our world.

I.

Searching

Matthew 18:12–14

"What is your opinion? If a man has a hundred sheep and one of them goes astray, will he not leave the ninety-nine in the hills and go in search of the stray? And if he finds it, amen, I say to you, he rejoices more over it than over the ninety-nine that did not stray. In just the same way, it is not the will of your heavenly Father that one of these little ones be lost."

God Seeks and We Resist

This parable surprises me. How many of us have spent most of our lives seeking God? I have. I'm sure many of you have too in one way or another. But what do we see here? We have God seeking us with abandon! To our human eyes and ears, this shepherd seems to do a foolish thing. He has a hundred sheep. When one of them is missing, he leaves the ninety-nine and goes in search of the lost one. And what does he do when he finds it?

He puts it on his shoulders, and, rejoicing, he brings the sheep home.

Strange? Disarming? What would happen if we stopped the intensity of our searching every once in a while and looked over our shoulder? What would we see? Would we be surprised to see God searching for us with more intensity than we could ever muster in our search for him? Ah, but how many of us truly want God to find us?

God is in constant pursuit of our hearts, but we are afraid of God finding us. At times, we feel his breath on our necks, and even though we know we can't escape, we still flee. As Saint Ignatius has said, God is everywhere and if we listen closely we can hear his call the way that lost sheep must have heard the call of his shepherd. God is in all things, in nature, in paintings, in motion pictures. He's also in people. Not just those whom we know in our lives—our family, our friends, the people we work with in the office—but in the strangers we read about in newspaper accounts when we're eating our breakfast. He's also present in the CNN Headline News we catch in the evening. He's in the eyes of billions of people around the world.

Why are many of us reluctant to be found, to be known and loved by this pervasive and searching God? Maybe we don't want to lose our freedom to God, the "tremendous lover." Maybe we think God will be angry at us for having left the flock. Maybe it's a matter of being afraid of responsibilities. Another reason for our wanting to flee God may be feelings of unworthiness. How many of us spend countless hours trying to impress people with our virtue without realizing that our so-called acts of niceness are ways of covering up the reality of our brokenness, our failures, our weakness? We don't want to surrender to God because we're afraid of being exposed for who we are. We build a castle around our inner, sinful, vulnerable self. We make a fort of walls and turrets. Our moats, arrows, and hot oil are ready for anyone who wants to get inside! At the center of the castle is a specially fortified room to which we will not grant access—not even to a most trusted lover. We're even reluctant to give access to God.

Some or all of these things may be true for us, but there is a depth of love that God the Father is hungering for us to enter into. A love that transcends the frailties of human love. In order to jump in, we need to surrender our fears. God is always seeking us, and we must turn and let him embrace us. We must acknowledge his love. Only when we stop, admit that the Father loves us, and then accept his love will we ever be free from the plight of having to prove our worthiness. Only when we turn and acknowledge our pursuer will we know God. Only then will we truly know ourselves.

Francis Thompson

The poet Francis Thompson (1859–1907) focused on this aspect of God the searcher in his poem "The Hound of Heaven." Thompson aspired to be a priest, but it was not to be. After a few months in the seminary he was asked to leave, and he went on to study to become a doctor. He failed three final examinations in medical school. Struggling with depression, he turned to morphine and was soon living in the crowded dirty back alleys of Victorian London. During one of his many failed attempts to rid himself of his addiction, he wrote "The Hound of Heaven." The poem tells of how he fled from God, of all the ways he tried to escape his Maker:

I fled Him down the nights and down the days;
I fled Him, down the arches of the years;
I fled Him, down the labyrinthine ways
Of my own mind; and in the midst of tears
I hid from Him, and under running laughter.
    Up vistaed hopes I sped;
    And shot, precipitated,
Adown Titanic glooms of chasmed fears,
From those strong Feet that followed, followed after.
    But with unhurried chase,
    And unperturbed pace,
    Deliberate speed, majestic instancy,
    They beat—and a Voice beat
    More constant than the Feet—
"All things betray thee who betrayest Me."

Feeling tired and knowing there is no escape, Thompson surrenders to the chasing hound:

    Now of that long pursuit
    Comes at hand the bruit;

That Voice is round me like a bursting sea:
   "And is thy earth so marred,
   Shattered in shard on shard?
   Lo, all things fly thee, for thou fliest Me!
   Strange, piteous, futile thing!
Wherefore should any set thee love apart?
Seeing none but I makes much of naught." (He said),
"And human love needs human meriting:
   How hast thou merited—
Of all man's clotted clay the dingiest clot?
   Alack, thou knowest not
How little worthy of any love thou art!
Whom will thou find to love ignoble thee,
Save Me, save only Me?"

All attempts to run away failed him. God was relentlessly, steadily, seeking him out, like a hound dog pursuing its prey. Through divine grace, coming out of deep depression and even despair, he admitted that God loved him. He surrendered himself, mind, body, and spirit. The poem's message to us is that by allowing ourselves to be captured, we gain the freedom of salvation.

Why Does God Seek Us?

These words are all fine and well, but many of us may not understand: Why exactly does God seek us like the shepherd seeks the lost sheep in the parable? What is it about us that God finds so attractive? Why risk abandoning the ninety-nine to find the one? When we're honest with ourselves—when we look at the wars around us, at our weaknesses, our repeated sins, our addictions, our fears, our failures, and our pride, our selfishness—why would God want to search for us?

Very mysterious!

But *not so mysterious* if we think of God as an artist. Unlike earthly artists who use paints and clay and music and dance to create their masterpieces, God's work is ongoing creations: the galaxy, a planet, a mountain, the wind, a lake, a flower. You and me. All are evolving, all are ever changing. And what is an artist looking for in his creation? Beauty. God as well is searching for the beauty in his creation. Certainly we are always evolving. Beauty seems to fade outwardly. Our body's cells are constantly changing, our skin and muscles move from firm to flabby, our hair changes color or falls out. But God sees past the surface of his paintings and sculptures; he sees the inner life of the creation. It's like going to a museum and looking at a painting. There is the surface experience. You see the colors and the shape of the subject, but there is an inner life to the picture in front of you, the life of the artist, the love of the artist that is bubbling below the surface. In many ways God's search for us is God's search for himself.

The Power of Freedom

Freedom is a significant part of what God has given us. It's the freedom of the lamb to wander off and get lost. God could have created us without this power. We could have lived lives that were forever unchanging, lives in which straying from the flock was never an option. Our freedom makes us exciting to God. He doesn't want his sheep to get lost. But if they do stray, he goes looking. The problem arises when we forget that God is ever seeking us! Oh, this forgetting that gets us into so much trouble.

God has given us freedom, and freedom by its very nature can bring unpredictable results. Will Adam and Eve eat the apple? Will the apostles ever leave the upper room? Will you and I turn and face God or will we turn away? Sure, God has a plan, a dream of what we should do, but he has surrendered the outcome to us. It's akin, in some ways, to listening to jazz musicians jamming in a nightclub. Freedom, like jazz, is unpredictable. A trumpet player may play a familiar riff in a song that everyone has heard countless times and then jump off into the unknown, leading the listener to uncharted territory. Good jazz, like real freedom, allows for a once-in-a-lifetime experience. Nothing is ever repeated in the same way twice.

The same unpredictability happens with writers too. Author Stephen King speaks of moments in the development of characters in his novels when the character takes over. All King does is follow the lead of his creation, allowing a fictional character to interact with other people, and from those interactions the formation of a plot evolves. The character the author created says and does things that Stephen King had never anticipated.

Our Drive for Happiness

Freedom, or the gift of free will, allows us to journey to self-realization. Think about it. The choices we make in many ways reveal what is important to us and sculpt who we become. We may not know at the time exactly what is motivating our choices, but it is our quest for happiness that prods us to do the things we do. Our hunger for joy is God's creative way of calling us to the dream he has for us, and God hopes that we will always be in his loving embrace. When we think of our quest for happiness, we might immediately think of comfort or riches or power. Those things can undeniably bring happiness, but on a deeper level our greatest moments of happiness come when we share God's gift of creation. When you think of times when you were truly happy, wasn't that happiness related to the joy of creating? Think of the happiness that is created when a couple conceives a child, a cook prepares a delicious dinner, a ballplayer hits a home run that wins the World Series, an author writes a book, a parent sees a child grow through a crisis, a comedian makes us laugh, or a doctor develops a medicine to help those with brain cancer. Happiness is intricately linked to creativity.

I know for me, happiness comes when I write a sermon or paint a picture. It also comes when I reconcile myself with an enemy, or develop a friendship, or make unbelievable moves while dancing at a wedding (I'm really light on my feet if I do say so myself). As we seek happiness through creation, God our Creator is seeking us right back and meeting us at every juncture. Yes, sometimes we find ourselves lost when our craving for happiness leads to selfishness, but the joy we derive from this parable, the true happiness we can find in these words of Jesus, is that God is never that far away. We may be lost, but if we look closely we can see the staff of our Father as the shepherd walks closer and closer to us and, reaching down, rescues us.

Prayer for Reflection

God, thank you for searching for me. Forgive me for running away from you. Help me to slow down and accept your love and realize the fullness of the dream you have for me now and forever in heaven.

QUESTIONS FOR DISCUSSION

1. How do we run away from God?
2. What will happen if we surrender to God?
3. How would we describe God's dream for us?
4. What brings us the most happiness?

2.

Humble

Luke 12:35–40

"Gird your loins and light your lamps and be like servants who await their master's return from a wedding, ready to open immediately when he comes and knocks. Blessed are those servants whom the master finds vigilant on his arrival. Amen, I say to you, he will gird himself, have them recline at table, and proceed to wait on them. And should he come in the second or third watch and find them prepared in this way, blessed are those servants."

The Tables Are Turned

As usual, Jesus catches us off guard with this powerful story and throws us a zinger. When the master comes and finds the servants ready, instead of putting them to work preparing something for him to eat, as we might expect, *the master has the servants sit down so that he can wait on them!*

What is Jesus trying to tell us here? The answer is

simple: If we are faithful in our service to God, if we keep our lamps burning like the vigilant servants in this parable, God the Master will respond by caring for us and serving us. This parable always evokes for me images of Jesus washing the feet of his disciples before the Passover meal on the evening before his death (John 13:5).

But getting back to the parable, look at how, with just a few words, Jesus throws out the window all the fearsome images of God the Father that have plagued many of us throughout our lives. The happy outcome of the story depends on keeping the flame lit until the master returns. What is this flame that the servants have to keep burning? And how exactly do we keep it burning?

Let's answer the first question. The flame is our faith in God. Although God's love for us is unconditional, he does have expectations of us. None of us is perfect, and certainly many of us fall. The light flickers and dims. Yet if we strive to believe in God and obey his commandments to love him with all our mind, heart, soul, and strength and then our neighbor as ourselves, that light will come back again. When we love, the light of God will shine through in everything we do.

Now, let's look at the second question. Practically speaking, how do we keep our light of faith in God alive? One way is to say yes to God. When you are asked by a friend or stranger, "Do you believe in God?" Answer with pride, "Yes!" Be proud to proclaim your faith when you recite the Nicene Creed during Mass. Tell others of your experiences with God. Download a sermon and listen to it.

Become conscious and aware of your actions. For instance, would the way you treat a coworker please God? Would the thought you have about a friend make God proud? What would God say about the anger you experience when you get behind the wheel of a car? Ask yourself, would God approve?

Then go deeper and with prayer in your heart increase the power of that light. We may wrestle with Jesus' challenge to love not only those we like and who like us, but our enemies as well. Give love to those who persecute you. Forgive the person who may have defamed you at your job. Forgive those who make jokes about you because of your religious beliefs. These are tough things to do, but we are called to forgive, forgive, forgive!

The Flame of Faith: God Believes in Me

Many times we may encounter a wind that tries to blow out the light, and this may manifest itself in our unbelief that God truly believes in us and wants the best of us. Do we believe, and have faith, that God loves us?

We can spend all our lives doing things to show God and others that we are people of faith and yet never believe that God truly loves us. John speaks of this when he writes in his first letter about the great sacrifice God made for us in Jesus. For us! "In this is love: not that we have loved God, but that he loved us and sent his Son as expiation for our sins" (1 John 4:10).

If we are unable to accept in faith God's love for us, we throw up a major obstacle to our being able to embrace him with the friendship and intimacy offered by the master described in the parable. Think of Peter, the apostle. How I want to shout with Peter when Jesus wants to wash his feet. Peter opens his mouth and says, "Lord, what do you mean that you want to serve me? You know my sins. You know my unfaithfulness."

"Yes, Peter!" says the master, "you were unfaithful, but I knew your regret at your failures. As flawed as you were, Peter, I saw your candle burning. Granted you have only a flicker of flame at times, but sit down, let me serve you. I so delight in being with you."

How many of us turn away from God's love? I know I have, and I still do from time to time, but if we let the force of this love settle in our souls, we may accept service from God. Yes, Lord, despite my repeated sins, despite my enslaving addictions, despite my following the other drummers of the world with their call to materialism, to sensuality and irresponsible freedom, Lord, I want to believe and accept your love for me. Lord, help my unbelief. Yes, Lord. Go ahead. Love me. Wash my feet if you must!

The Humble Servant

As I've already mentioned, the face of God the Father serving us can seem strange, especially if our faith has been

formed with the idea that God is distant and judgmental.
Yet here in this parable we see the Father acting as the humble servant. More evidence of this can be found in the book
of Genesis, where the Lord cares for our needs by creating
everything we could possibly want. He keeps us warm with
the sun; he caresses us with the cooling wind; we have our
food and drink from plants and animals; water cleanses and
refreshes us; the colors of the seasons delight our eyes; and
we share in creation through the gift of sexuality. We see
this yet again in the New Testament as the humble servant
sends his only Son to become one of us, for our salvation,
signifying in the process that God is humble.

As we reflect on God's humility we need to remember
our call to be humble servants as well. If God our Creator
is humble and willing to serve us, how could we ever strive
to be anything less?

Concentrating on the Flame

As we've already discussed, keeping the fire alive is quite
a task. The parable's simple call to give all our attention to
the flame speaks to us of the importance of concentration.

Let's face it. Our lives are filled with distractions. We
set out to do something very important. Then the phone
rings. Then there's a knock at the door. Then our stom-
ach growls and we head for the refrigerator. Then a picture
comes up on our screen saver and we're off to the world
of reverie. Then we sit down for ten minutes and try to

remember what was so important before our chain of distractions set in. Wait! What were we talking about? Oh, yes, concentration! The flame!

Several years ago I came across a book called *The Inner Game of Tennis*, in which the author, Timothy Gallwey, speaks convincingly of how to concentrate on living in the here and now. Gallwey used the image of a tennis ball to make an important point. In the middle of a game, the only thing you have to be concerned with is the ball. You watch it as your opponent bends to bounce and catch it. You watch it thrown into the air and then see it meet the racket and come sailing toward you. While it is in flight you try to notice the rotation of the lines of the ball. As it approaches, you let the ball dictate the position of your body and feet. The grip of the racket is secondary. You just meet the ball now.

If I had only followed his advice I could have made it to Wimbledon. I wish! My problem, aside from a flat left foot and an ungainly inner tube at my waist, is my debilitating lack of concentration. Instead of losing myself in the here and now, in the ball coming to me, I am preoccupied with the foolish move I made during the last point or concerned with whether I'll be able to start my temperamental car after the game.

The challenge at the center of the parable is to focus our concentration on the flame before us in a way similar to what Gallwey talks about in his book. We need to pay attention to the present moment and let go of the debilitating preoccupation with the past and the future. We are called

upon to let go of the anxiety and the worry in our lives. This
is possible because of our confidence in the Father's love
for us. In this secure place we can relax. There's nothing
more important in the Father's dream for us than responding to the now with faith, hope, and love.

This letting go of worry is what Jesus is talking about
when he says:

> *"Therefore I tell you, do not worry about your life and*
> *what you will eat, or about your body and what you*
> *will wear. For life is more than food and the body more*
> *than clothing. Notice the ravens: they do not sow or*
> *reap; they have neither storehouse nor barn, yet God*
> *feeds them. How much more important are you than*
> *birds! Can any of you by worrying add a moment to your*
> *life-span? If even the smallest things are beyond your*
> *control, why are you anxious about the rest?"* (Luke
> 12:22–26)

God is saying, Now, this moment, is all I want you to concentrate on. I don't want you spending your time worrying about five minutes ago or five days ago. You can't do
anything about then. And I want you to let go of your ap-
prehension about five seconds from now, five minutes, five
days, or five years from now. Do well what you are doing at
this moment. That's all I require.

Now Is the Creative Moment

Not only is concentrating on the flame of faith the key to living a good life with God and others; it also offers you the freedom and incentive to create. Now is the moment of greatness! Now is the start of the dream you've always been too distracted to begin. Center on the flame of faith before you. It's all that matters. Think of the wonders people have created by responding to the now. At one second in time, Beethoven wrote the first note of his Fifth Symphony, Van Gogh laid the first dab of paint on the canvas that became his self-portrait, and Tolstoy wrote the first word of the novel *War and Peace*. They all started in the now. Imagine the flood of power-packed nows that lie before you. Grab one and confidently move into the greatness of God's dream for you.

Do good and keep the flame alive with your love of the Father. Serve God. Then relax as he humbly serves you.

Prayer for Reflection

God, thank you for being a humble servant. I have to change spiritual gears to comprehend your love. It's amazing that you want to serve me. I accept your love. Stay with me in all the nows of my life. Help me to keep the flame alive.

QUESTIONS FOR DISCUSSION

1. How can we be humble?
2. Do you believe God loves you?
3. How do you show your faith to others?
4. If we were to let go of anxiety about the past and future and embrace the now, what magnificent thing could we do?

3.

Listening

Luke 18:2–5

"There was a judge in a certain town who neither feared God nor respected any human being. And a widow in that town used to come to him and say, 'Render a just decision for me against my adversary.' For a long time the judge was unwilling, but eventually he thought, 'While it is true that I neither fear God nor respect any human being, because this widow keeps bothering me I shall deliver a just decision for her lest she finally come and strike me.'"

Using Humor to Make His Point

I bet that the people laughed out loud when they heard this parable. Here's a poor, defenseless widow going up against a formidable, godless judge, and, surprise ending, she wins. Why? Because he's afraid that she's going to strike him. I love it! We laugh and cheer for the underdog.

Through this humorous story Jesus is bringing home to the crowds who were listening to him the point he makes elsewhere in the Gospels with sharp clarity: "[A]sk and you will receive; seek and you will find; knock and the door will be opened to you. For everyone who asks, receives; and the one who seeks, finds; and to the one who knocks, the door will be opened" (Luke 11:9–10). And again Jesus says, "Amen, amen, I say to you, whatever you ask the Father in my name he will give you" (John 16:23).

Jesus knows that along with clearly making his point in simple, understandable words, the best way of getting his message into our heads is by jarring us with a parable. It's like he's saying, "If you're not going to believe in the Father's desire to listen to your needs and then grant you what you wish when I tell you with clear words, then listen to this funny story and learn."

· Jesus knew that a well-crafted, humorous story is a vital ingredient in a speech. A story, especially if it has humor, is what the audience remembers. In this story Jesus compares his loving and generous Father to a godless, stingy judge who is begrudgingly forced to make a just decision. The judge may be a tough character, but he seems to be a good listener, and in the end we see the twist when Jesus concludes the tale with a surprise—a judge cowers and a pugnacious widow gets what she wanted.

Types of Prayer

So how can we interpret this parable today? One way is to look at the widow's repeated requests as prayers. Jesus calls us to pray to the Father, and in this parable the woman calls out to the man in authority. When she doesn't get a response, does she give up? Nope, she asks again. So let us take a few moments and reflect on some of the ways we can and should pray with insistence. The acronym ACTS sums up four key forms of prayer: Adoration, Contrition, Thanksgiving, and Supplication.

ADORATION

In adoration we praise God with words of love and admiration: "God, I praise you for your wisdom and your care for us. The wealth of your creation is overwhelming, in the mountains, the sea, and the desert. Praise to you for trees and plants. Praise to you for the wonder of us human beings."

CONTRITION

In this type of prayer we offer words of repentance and express remorse and sorrow for our faults and bad actions: "Lord, I know I have sinned. I've fallen short of the mark. I've left the path that you have shown me with your example in Jesus' life and your commandments. My conscience is calling out to me to change, to turn away from my sin. Please, Lord, forgive me."

THANKSGIVING

A prayer of thanksgiving is one that doesn't just have to happen around the holidays. It can, and should, be a daily exercise by which we express gratitude and show appreciation for all our blessings: "Lord, thank you for my life. Thank you for the people who are part of my life. Thank you for the dreams and talents you have given me. Thank you for the difficulties and sufferings I experience. Thank you for the gift of faith in you."

SUPPLICATION

In the last form of prayer we petition God and bring our needs to him (just like the widow did with the judge). "Lord, I need your help. The doctor has just told me that I have cancer. Please, Lord, cure this disease. Please, please, please help me."

It is this prayer of supplication that we are going to look at more closely now.

God's Response: A Call to Intimacy

The parable has two parts. The widow petitions and the judge responds. Along with going to the Father with our many petitions, we should think of what God's response will be. Are we prepared for any answer? Are we prepared for silence?

Any communication with the Father is a call to deep intimacy. Saint Paul explains this intimacy in terms of the indwelling of God the Holy Spirit. "The Spirit of God dwells in you" (Romans 8:9). Paul says that this intimacy is so intense that God the Holy Spirit prays for us when we don't know how to pray:

> *In the same way, the Spirit too comes to the aid of*
> *our weakness; for we do not know how to pray as we*
> *ought, but the Spirit itself intercedes with inexpressible*
> *groanings. And the one who searches hearts knows*
> *what is the intention of the Spirit, because it intercedes*
> *for the holy ones according to God's will. (Romans*
> *8:26–27)*

All this being said, I must confess that I have a serious problem with the Father's response to many of my prayers. Let me share with you a story.

Some years back, early on in my priesthood, I was teaching religion at a high school in Los Angeles, explaining to a class of teenagers how great God is. I used the adjectives "all-powerful," "all-present," and "all-knowing." When the bell rang for lunch, one of the students asked if he could talk with me. He had a question. "Father, you talk about how God is all those *all*s, and then you want us to talk to God and get close to him, to be intimate. My problem is with God being 'all-knowing.' To be honest with you, I don't like a know-it-all."

Nice point. I gulped and tried to cover my surging

panic. I understood where the student was coming from because I, too, did all I could to avoid know-it-alls. They're obnoxious! I feel very self-conscious around them, and I'm afraid of expressing anything to them for fear of being told I'm wrong! I don't want to communicate with them. I realized I didn't like know-it-alls either, and there I was, saying God was all-knowing and expecting my students to want to come close and even become intimate with God.

I can't remember how I answered my student. I wasn't very convincing. He gave me an incredulous look and went off to his lunch. Yet the experience shook me. The student's question became like a haunting melody that kept playing in my mind.

Intimacy Involves Change

The teachings of Jesus call for our prayer to be a natural part of an intimate relationship with God. Jesus says, "I pray not only for them, but also for those who will believe in me through their word, so that they may all be one, as you, Father, are in me and I in you, that they also may be in us, that the world may believe that you sent me" (John 17:21). You can't get more intimate than that.

Intimate relationships of friendship and love involve a certain degree of vulnerability. They also involve communication. There's dialogue—give-and-take—with more giving than taking if one wants success in the relationship.

The product of this exchange is emotional and spiritual growth. And growth, by its very nature, involves change.

The Intimacy Problem

But now we face a problem. God doesn't change as I learned in my grade-school education from the Baltimore Catechism, lesson 2, #12: "God is all-knowing." Heaven knows it's tough to get close to a human know-it-all. But what about God, who's a real know-it-all? If God knows the past, the present, and the future, there really isn't much room for a growing intimacy, is there? He knows everything about me. When I pray to an all-knowing God, am I just going through the motions? He knows what I'm going to say even before I say it.

Under these conditions, would there ever be a chance that God could change his mind? Is it possible, if I present my case to God with a lot of passion and reason, that God would be willing to change the course of the universe after hearing my argument?

In the book of Genesis, Abraham has a conversation with God after hearing of the Lord's dissatisfaction with the cities of Sodom and Gomorrah. He asks God: "Suppose there were fifty innocent people in the city; would you wipe out the place, rather than spare it for the sake of the fifty innocent people within it?" (Genesis 18:24). God listens, and his response is that he is indeed open to changing his mind. We smile as we hear Abraham slide the number of good people to forty-five, then forty, then thirty, then twenty, then ten. Unfortunately ten good people couldn't be found, so the cities were destroyed. *But there was a healthy conversation.* There was listening and there were concessions.

In the ninth chapter of Deuteronomy we hear the story of the Jewish people wandering in the desert and insulting God by making a golden calf and worshipping it. Yahweh was incensed. He decided to wipe out all his people. Moses had a conversation with God. He argued that if God were to do that the Egyptians would laugh at God because he would have failed with the people he had saved from slavery. God changed his mind. Imagine that! God had a plan and Moses talked him out of it.

These two instances, not to mention the parable that Jesus teaches us in the beginning of this chapter, convince me that even though God may be all-knowing, this does not impede our journey to conversation and intimacy. The real question is, are we open to the Father's response?

How Does God Respond?

If we're open to God's listening and then responding with openness to change, how exactly does he answer? Jesus says to us:

> *"Which one of you would hand his son a stone when he asks for a loaf of bread, or a snake when he asks for*

a fish? If you then, who are wicked, know how to give
good gifts to your children, how much more will your
heavenly Father give good things to those who ask him?"
(Matthew 7:9–11)

In my experiences this is true. I've seen important—and
sometimes dramatic—changes happen after prayer. Can-
cers are cured. Broken relationships are healed. Depression is lifted. Sometimes a person enslaved by an addiction
finds the strength to change the direction of her life. These
things may seem like impossibilities now, but for God "all
things are possible" (Matthew 19:26).

When Prayers Are Not Answered

Jesus uses the parable of the godless judge and the widow
to show us the Father's desire to answer our prayers. But if
this is true, why do so many of our prayers go unanswered?
"I prayed for my baby's cancer to be healed, but she died."
"I prayed to find a marriage partner, but here I am in my
eighties and alone." "I prayed for your help when the hur-
ricane was coming, but, look, I lost my husband in our
flooded house."

We can respond to these situations with faith or no
faith. Do we believe in God's love or not? Our response
depends on the direction of our heart. Without this faith,
God can often appear to be a cruel, uncaring cause of evil.
With faith in God's love for us, we see his faithful response

to us even when tragedies occur. Even when we're not getting what we ask for, with the eyes of faith we see God working in a powerful way to bless us and those we love. There is the old saying that the Lord works in mysterious ways. And so he does. The death of a mother may move a wayward son to seek help for his drinking problem. An abused wife who suffers a broken arm may find the courage to move away from a husband who beats her up regularly. All we need do in our times of trouble and even tragedy is turn around and look at God with faith. He can turn our problems into blessings.

Saint Paul had his share of injustice, tragedies, and persecution. In his Second letter to the Corinthians 11:25–27 he says, "Five times at the hands of the Jews I received forty lashes minus one. Three times I was beaten with rods, once I was stoned, three times I was shipwrecked, I passed a night and a day on the deep; on frequent journeys, in dangers from rivers, dangers from robbers, dangers from my own race, dangers from Gentiles, dangers in the city, dangers in the wilderness, dangers at sea, dangers among false brothers; in toil and hardship, through many sleepless nights, through hunger and thirst, through frequent fastings, through cold and exposure."

Paul certainly had grounds for denying God's love and even his existence. But because he had experienced God's love for him, he was able to say, "We know that all things work for good for those who love God" (Romans 8:28).

We are called to enter into dialogue with God, but at the same time we are called to surrender to faith in God's love. With confidence in his call to intimacy I say: "God, I don't understand. Why don't you always break into my world with healing during times of illness? I don't comprehend why at times you can't fully protect me from the troubles of this world. Those instances leave me confused, angry, and sometimes overcome with helplessness. But then your love stirs in my soul. I believe in your love. You care for me more than the godless judge in the parable. You answer my prayers in your own way with the assurance of blessings, even in tragedies. I hear your promise of life now and for all eternity. Thank you for the gift of your love. Strengthen my faith."

Try It

Let God be more than an implacable One who doesn't care about what you want. Let God love you! Let him be enriched by you, his creation. Imagine him being anxious to hear what you have to say. Listen for his answer. Be open to it. Take his answer and come back with a new response, which can be off the top of your head or studied. It can be said with a smile or a tear. It can be endearing or brimming with anger. Go ahead. Talk with God. Have a conversation. God has a listening face.

Prayer for Reflection

> *God, draw me into a deep, intimate conversation with you*
> *both when I pray by myself and when I pray with others.*
> *Help me to trust that you are willing to have an honest*
> *dialogue with me. Help me to believe in the unbelievable*
> *wonders you do because of my prayer. Sustain me when I*
> *have problems hearing your response.*

QUESTIONS FOR DISCUSSION

1. Explain what goes on when you talk with God.
2. When, where, and how do you pray?
3. How does God answer your prayers?
4. How do you deal with unanswered prayers?
5. Is God willing to change his mind if you ask him to?

4.

Giving

Matthew 13:44–46

"The kingdom of heaven is like a treasure buried in a field, which a person finds and hides again, and out of joy goes and sells all that he has and buys that field. Again, the kingdom of heaven is like a merchant searching for fine pearls. When he finds a pearl of great price, he goes and sells all that he has and buys it."

God Is Our Pearl

Immediately on hearing this parable we compare the treasure buried in the field and the pearl of great price to God. Pretty simple, right? When we find God in our lives, we find a treasure, a precious pearl. And we can experience this gift in many different ways: in the Bible, at Mass, in the love of others, and in the realization that at the center of all creation is an expectant God waiting for us to enter his heart.

But let's for a moment turn the tables a bit. What if, as

an exercise, we looked at the parable in a new way? What if, instead of God being the treasure and the pearl, it was you and I who took on that role? We become the buried treasure that is found, the pearl of great price, and God gives up all he has to buy us.

Let the wonder of that sink in.

We are great treasures to God. We are priceless in God's eyes. And God will give anything to have us.

The strongest evidence of this can be found in Jesus. God the Father loved us so much, was so taken by the pearl of humanity, that he gave us his Son Jesus so that we might be with him forever. When we look at the parable in this way, we may shake our heads in disbelief. How could the Father give us his Son, his only Son, for us? How could he endanger his most precious possession? What if we didn't treat his Son with love and respect? What if we rejected him? (How could he risk his Son in this way?)

Love.

And this love is expressed to us in Jesus' words of prayer explaining the giving face of his Father who desires us so much:

> *"And I have given them the glory you gave me, so that they may be one, as we are one, I in them and you in me, that they may be brought to perfection as one, that the world may know that you sent me, and that you loved them even as you loved me." (John 17:22–23)*

Those are potent words. The Father loves us as much as he loves Jesus.

Jesus says he has come to save all those the Father has given him:

> *"I revealed your name to those whom you gave me out*
> *of the world. They belonged to you, and you gave them*
> *to me, and they have kept your word . . . I pray for*
> *them . . . because they are yours, and everything of mine*
> *is yours and everything of yours is mine, and I have been*
> *glorified in them." (John 17:6, 9–10)*

Moreover, not only did God give us Jesus so that we could be with God for all eternity; he also gave us the Holy Spirit, the Father's ongoing gift to show us his love. Jesus assured his disciples (and reassures us) that although he was going to leave them in body, he was leaving behind the Holy Spirit to live with us and reveal and remind us of the teachings of Jesus:

> *"But when he comes, the Spirit of truth, he will guide*
> *you to all truth. He will not speak on his own, but he*
> *will speak what he hears, and will declare to you the*
> *things that are coming. He will glorify me, because*
> *he will take from what is mine and declare it to you.*
> *Everything that the Father has is mine; for this reason I*
> *told you that he will take from what is mine and declare*
> *it to you." (John 16:13–15)*

All these teachings call us to life with the Father now, and for all eternity in heaven.

Our Response to the Father's Love

What should our response be if God loves us as much as he does? The answer is simple (though as human history has proven, difficult to carry out): We should each strive to return that love with as much love and surrender as we can muster.

Now, you might be saying, Father Mike, that's all well and good, but how do I do that, practically speaking? I want to love God, but I don't know how to do it.

Let's look at the words of Christ for an answer. One way that Jesus defines love is in terms of keeping the commandments:

> *"Whoever has my commandments and observes them is the one who loves me. And whoever loves me will be loved by my Father, and I will love him and reveal myself to him." (John 14:21)*

We might want a more emotional response to how God wants us to manifest our love for him. But no, God is practical. The commandments are pretty concrete, literally! God gave the Ten Commandments to Moses written on stone. You can't cut and paste a commandment. If God based our love only on emotions it could be as rootless and fluctuating as our moods.

The Ten Commandments are clear and they are un-changeable:

1. Love God more than fame, money, and selfish pleasure.
2. Let God's name be uttered only with reverence.
3. Set aside one day a week to rest and worship God.
4. Honor your parents. Take good care of them.
5. Don't kill anybody with a gun or your tongue.
6. Be faithful to those you love.
7. Don't steal.
8. Don't lie.
9. Don't keep looking for things to make you happy.
10. Don't yearn for other people to make you happy.

Now, that's a pretty healthy to-do (or not-to-do) list, but Jesus reminds us in his summation of these commandments that love must come first. The greatest commandment, the great summation, is love God and your neighbor as yourself.

Yet for Jesus this was just the beginning, a launching pad, for journeying to God. Certainly, one must keep God's commandments, yet Jesus challenged us to go deeper, to carry these laws not just on our tongues, but in our hearts. Yes, we should not murder, but Jesus says we shouldn't even get angry. Yes, we should not commit adultery, but Jesus says don't even lust after someone. Jesus takes the commandments from the physical to the mental—to the mind. When Jesus says, "So be perfect, just as your heavenly Father is perfect" (Matthew 5:48), he is saying perfect your mind and your soul first because that's where all action originates. God wants us to go deeper!

This desire to go further, to go beyond just the minimum, ties in with my lifelong desire to be a priest. When I was very young I knew I wanted to give more to God, to go beyond an ordinary existence with him, and I surrendered my life to the Lord by taking vows of poverty, chastity, and obedience.

I mention my response to God not to imply that my life is better than another person's. Each of us is called to accept this giving face of God in his or her own way, as best as we can. This might be through marriage and a family. A person may choose to be single and dedicate his or her life to a vocation of some sort. But to whatever life we are called, we are meant to go deeper into our relationship with God and others. For a married person, it means going beyond the surface of just two people in love. It means descending into the mysterious depths of love for another.

Now, our different responses to God can cause a bit of anxiety. One person may compare himself to another and feel like he is coming up short. Saint Paul understood this, and we can use his words to set our minds at ease, to help us to realize that each and every one of us is an important part of God's creation:

> But as it is, God placed the parts, each one of them, in
> the body as he intended. If they were all one part, where
> would the body be? But as it is, there are many parts,
> yet one body. The eye cannot say to the hand, "I do not

need you," nor again the head to the feet, "I do not need you." (1 Corinthians 12:18–21)

I love this passage because it reminds us that we need to listen to the Father—the great giver—and answer his call to intimacy. Each of us is important. Each of us is precious like a pearl, like a great treasure, and God continues to give us so much in exchange for our love.

Prayer for Reflection

God, thank you for your personal love for me. Sometimes I find it hard to imagine that you consider me as a pearl and treasure for whom you have given your Son. Strengthen my faith in your tender love for me. Help me to see your love in nature, and especially in the people you bring into my life.

QUESTIONS FOR DISCUSSION

1. How would you describe your relationship with Jesus?
2. Would you give all that you had for God? Explain your answer.
3. Give examples of people who have given their lives for various treasures and pearls.
4. Do you really believe that God sees you as a pearl and a treasure? Why or why not?
5. What are the minimum things we have to do to gain heaven?

5.

Celebrating

Matthew 22:2–10

"The kingdom of heaven may be likened to a king who gave a wedding feast for his son. He dispatched his servants to summon the invited guests to the feast, but they refused to come. A second time he sent other servants, saying, 'Tell those invited: Behold, I have prepared my banquet, my calves and fattened cattle are killed, and everything is ready; come to the feast.' Some ignored the invitation and went away, one to his farm, another to his business. The rest laid hold of his servants, mistreated them, and killed them. The king was enraged and sent his troops, destroyed those murderers, and burned their city. Then he said to his servants, 'The feast is ready, but those who were invited were not worthy to come. Go out, therefore, into the main roads and invite to the feast whomever you find.' The servants went out into the streets and gathered all they found, bad and good alike, and the hall was filled with guests."

A Cause for Celebration

The parable of the king throwing a wedding party for his son is a powerful story that highlights a very complex picture of who the Father is. Here Jesus is telling us that God is a celebratory God. Life is a celebration, and the Father is excited to share with us the food and drink he has prepared. It's as if God is saying, "Come, come to my celebration. This will be a party you'll never forget." How exciting. Who doesn't like a party? Whether it's a wedding feast with hundreds of people or a birthday party for two with the person you love more than anything in this world.

I can distinctly recall a memorable celebration that was pivotal in my life. On a cold day in January 1969, in Illinois, I was ordained a priest. That day was the culmination of fourteen years of seminary study. Sitting with me in the sanctuary of the church were my mom and dad. I have a picture on my fireplace of the bishop laying his hands on my head. That was the official moment of ordination. Thus did a dream come true.

After the ordination service I met with my family and friends in a room near the chapel. Now, forty years later, I can remember so many details of the day. My sister Mary, my sister Alice with her seven kids, my brother Bill and his eight children, aunts and uncles, and my cousins Larry and Les were present.

Then, in the evening, all my classmates, with their

families and friends, gathered in the large seminary dining room for a ham dinner. Mom and Dad were sitting across from me. This was the end of a long day. When I looked over at Mom, I realized something was wrong. I knew she was exhausted, but this was more serious. She froze and then started shaking. I don't remember if I went over or under the table, but I got to her and laid her on the floor. I reached into her mouth and pulled out some of the ham she'd been eating. My sister Mary was right there with a nitro pill to place under Mom's tongue to keep her heart pumping. An ambulance came quickly, and we drove to the hospital with sirens blaring. I was terrified and prayed throughout the night. The next morning we found out that Mom was going to be all right, and that news was a reason to rejoice! Within twenty-four hours I had experienced two very different kinds of celebration, but at the center of each for me was the preciousness of God's gift of life to us.

A Surprising Face of God

A party is something many of us find familiar and heart-warming. A person lives another year. That's an accomplishment. Let's have a birthday party, and let's save a chair for God while we're at it. A team wins a championship. Let's break out the champagne. A young woman finally graduates from college. Let's all get together and raise a toast to her future. A couple is married and joined together for life. Let's dance! As a nation we thank God for our Founding

Fathers and Mothers on the Fourth of July. We celebrate the memory of those who have fought and died for us. We take a day off work and remember the accomplishments of Abraham Lincoln and Martin Luther King, Jr.

As people of faith we appreciate the fullness of life to which the celebrating face of the Father calls us. Our faith is not something that restricts us with legalism (even if we do acknowledge that God has built rules into nature to guide us). No, our faith is something that opens us up to happiness and fullness of life. We eat together and drink together and participate in the love that moves all of creation.

As Catholics we find the face of God every week in a celebration of song, contrition, praise, Bible reading, and then a meal of the Body and the Blood of Jesus—the Mass. This meal is the gift Christ gave us at his last celebration with his disciples the evening before his death. Yet this communion is just one of seven very special celebrations in which we can encounter God in an intimate way. These celebrations constitute key moments in our lives and sustain us on our journey to God. We call these moments of encounter with God the seven sacraments: baptism, Eucharist, reconciliation, confirmation, marriage, ordination to the priesthood, and anointing of the sick.

God's Signs of Love

Sacraments are a way of glimpsing the beautiful face of the Father, and they are a way of entering into the mystery of love. Imagine for a moment the love a husband has for his wife. He loves this woman with every ounce of his being, but he always experiences a frustration in being able to express his love. He says the words "I love you," but then shakes his head in disappointment. Those words don't encompass what's in his heart. So he pulls out a love poem and hopes that the poet will help him come closer to the meaning of his true love. He may even put the poem to music. But the words and music are never enough. So next he'll make an expression on his face. No words. It's a sincere expression of longing and tender intimacy through vulnerable eyes. A deep sigh comes out of his mouth. Great but still not enough. Then he turns to things: roses, perfume, jewelry, clothes, a car, a meal at a fancy restaurant . . . Again, lovely, but these things don't express the enormity of the love he feels for his beloved. Words, facial expressions, physical things are all symbols we use to express what's in our hearts. The reality of love is always more than can be expressed. No matter how hard you try, you can't seem to articulate the intensity of the love in your heart. How does that make you feel?

Now imagine what God goes through to show his love for us. He tries and tries to shower us with affection, but it's so hard for us, the beloved, to understand just how grand that love is. He gives us water. He gives us bread. He gives us forgiveness. He gives us power. He gives us love. He gives us commitment. He gives us healing and relief. And still we may not understand just how much God cares for us.

Aware of the need for signs to express the enormity of God's love for us in the sacrament, the Church celebrates the ordinary to show this relentless love, through sacramentals. Water, which we use to clean and refresh ourselves, now becomes the means God uses to cleanse and refresh us spiritually through baptism. A candle, which saves us from stumbling in the dark, becomes an experience of God's direction and protection in our life. Oil, which we use to protect us from the sun, lubricate creaking bones, and which can cause explosions in our car that can speed us down the highway, now becomes a sacred symbol to protect, lubricate, and fire us up with his Spirit. Incense rising up to heaven reminds us of prayers going up to God and delights our noses. Words from Scripture are symbols of God's passionate love for us.

Public Celebrations of God

Beyond individual sacraments, the heart of all religious celebrations is public prayer and worship. Although for many of us a formal commitment to God might have happened when we were young, we need to acknowledge our belief in God on a regular basis to assure growth in our relationship with him. Attending church services is a celebratory act of love. The requirement for a weekly public acknowledgment of God's love is akin to the need of husbands and wives to physically and verbally express their love on a regular basis. To neglect these expressions by going for long times without saying and showing love leads to the death of feeling. We can be busy with all kinds of important and good works, but if we don't work to foster the love and friendships in our lives we're missing one of life's basic ingredients for survival.

Not only does God deserve this weekly acknowledgment, but we need the support of our fellow worshippers. And they need our support as well. Following God's way can be lonely. We can be in a family, a school, a workplace, a neighborhood where we feel all alone. We need the presence of other believers to strengthen us to go on. When we're celebrating God with other believers, we are strengthened to continue our charge of loving God and others after the celebration.

Freedom from Ruts

Many of us fall into the ruts of habit in our spiritual lives. Celebrations call us out of our routines to see ourselves and others in a new light. We can so easily be absorbed in the problems of living together in our family. Our relatives can make us uncomfortable with their idiosyncrasies, their demands, their fears, and their selfishness. Our work can overwhelm us with deadlines, meetings, competition, and budgets. Celebrations help us not to take people for granted.

Celebrations allow us to move from the ordinary to the extraordinary. We stop. We look around. We relax. We see people in a new light. We transcend the details to find the bigger picture, the dream that motivated us in the first place to enter into the marriage or the job. Celebrations re-invigorate. They give us a new understanding of our lives.

The Face of God: The Life of the Party

Imagine God knocking at your door. As you open the door you see him standing with a big grin on his face. "Come to my place, will you. We're getting together with friends. There's good food, music, and dancing. We're going to sit around and tell those stories that we love to hear. Please come. I'm counting on you. We'll forget all our troubles. We'll laugh and cry. We'll let our hair down. The main thing is that I want to tell you, in front of everybody, how much I love you. Will you come?"

That would be quite a face to see. Am I being fanciful? I think not. If the invitation of the king in the parable means anything, it means that God is welcoming us to a feast, a feast of new life.

We should accept the invitation.

The Promise of the Celebration of Heaven

Scripture tells us of an end-of-time banquet. Isaiah 25:6 speaks of an extraordinary feast at which all will participate. The mountain he speaks of is, for us Christians, the heavenly Jerusalem: "On this mountain the LORD of hosts will provide for all peoples a feast of rich food and choice wines, juicy, rich food and pure, choice wines."

As I strive to follow God's will and grow in my love of him, the thought of the face of the celebrating Father and his invitation to celebrate with him for all eternity permeates my faith. What a delight. When we celebrate today, we both anticipate and join in the reality of heaven in the here and now.

Prayer for Reflection

God, help me to enter into the celebration of your love for me and my love for you. Deepen my love for you, Lord. Help me to rejoice more with my family, friends, and those with whom I work. Fill me with a burning desire and longing to celebrate with you and those I love forever in heaven.

QUESTIONS FOR DISCUSSION

1. Describe the best celebration you ever had. Why was it so special?
2. Why are celebrations important?
3. Can you imagine God celebrating with you? What would he do?
4. Jesus talks about inviting the poor, blind, and homeless to your celebrations. Can you do that at your next party? How?

6.

Loving

Luke 10:30–35

"A man fell victim to robbers as he went down from Jerusalem to Jericho. They stripped and beat him and went off leaving him half-dead. A priest happened to be going down that road, but when he saw him, he passed by on the opposite side. Likewise a Levite came to the place, and when he saw him, he passed by on the opposite side. But a Samaritan traveler who came upon him was moved with compassion at the sight. He approached the victim, poured oil and wine over his wounds and bandaged them. Then he lifted him up on his own animal, took him to an inn and cared for him. The next day he took out two silver coins and gave them to the innkeeper with the instruction, 'Take care of him. If you spend more than what I have given you, I shall repay you on my way back,'"

Finding God Quickly

For many of us, if we wanted to look on God's face right now we would go to a place of worship or we would look to the people we've designated as God people: priests, ministers, rabbis, mullahs, nuns, deacons, or even people volunteering in churches. This is where Jesus went to look for God. As a young boy of twelve Jesus went to the Temple and talked with the people who were connected with his Father's house. Years later, as a grown man, he protected the sanctity of his Father's house by driving out the people who were making the Temple a place of business and not a place of reverent prayer.

Yet we see in the parable that there is another place where God resides, and that place is the hearts of the people who need our help. The parable shows us that a person can see the face of God by ministering to someone who is lying on the side of the road. Yet what is ironic in this story is that those who would consider themselves close to God pass by a dying man as they rush to take care of other matters. In their failure to help the man who had been brutalized by thieves, these men fail to look into the eyes of God. The true godly act is done by a Samaritan man, who is not welcome in the Jerusalem Temple, a man who is seen to be part of a race that is distant from God the Father.

Who Are the Characters?

But let's take a step back. In order to come to a deeper understanding of this parable, let's put the story in a historical context so that we can better imagine the impact Jesus' words had on his listeners.

Priests in the first century A.D. were descendants in the line starting with Aaron, who was made high priest after Moses led the Israelites out of Egypt. The priests were men chosen to perform sacred acts in the Temple. By the time of Jesus, over a thousand years after the Exodus, priests were still considered special people in God's eyes.

Priests such as Zechariah, the husband of Elizabeth and the father of John the Baptist, offered incense as a way of ushering prayers to heaven. They sacrificed the lambs at the altar of the Temple on special feasts like the Passover. They also would sacrifice doves, the offering of choice for poorer people who couldn't afford the more expensive lamb. We see this in the Gospel of Luke when Mary came to the Temple for her purification after the birth of her son:

> *When the days were completed for their purification according to the law of Moses, they took him up to Jerusalem to present him to the Lord, just as it is written in the law of the Lord, "Every male that opens the womb shall be consecrated to the Lord," and to offer the sacrifice of "a pair of turtledoves or two young pigeons," in accordance with the dictate in the law of the Lord. (Luke 2:22–24)*

Yet, regardless of the animal used, sacrifice was a way of showing love for God, and offering up the sacrifice was, for priests, a very important job.

While most priests in the Jewish tradition were from the line of Levi, not every Levite was a priest. As Bible scholar John McKenzie pointed out, "The distinction between the priests and the Levites establishes the Levites as inferior ministers who assist the priests and perform sacred but not sacerdotal functions in the sanctuary" (*Dictionary of the Bible*, 504). Yet regardless of the role an individual Levite played, members of the house of Levi were entrusted with educating the Hebrews about worship and adoration of God.

Now, let's look at the other important character in this story. The Samaritan was a resident of Samaria, a mountainous area some ten miles south of Nazareth. Samaria had formerly been the land of the kings of the northern kingdom, Israel. Tragedy came to these prosperous people when an army from the north, the area of present-day Iraq, called the Assyrians, conquered the Samaritans some seven hundred years before the birth of Jesus. Over 25,000 Samaritans were relocated across the Middle East as slaves. Some Samaritans remained in their land to farm and pay taxes to the Assyrians, but the Assyrians also brought slaves from other countries they had conquered to live in Samaria. By the time the Assyrians had been conquered and the dispersed Samaritans could return home, many of the Jews of Samaria had intermarried with non-Jews.

Because of their mixed blood, the Samaritans were shunned by the Jews of Jerusalem. As a way of rebelling against the status quo, these people chose to follow only the Pentateuch (the first five books of the Old Testament), and they set up their own place of worship on a mountain called Gerizim because they were not welcome in Jerusalem's Temple. The Jews faithful to the Temple of Jerusalem considered the Samaritans heretics.

So here is the situation. Two seemingly special people of God pass up the opportunity to help a seriously injured man. Instead a heretic, a person considered by Jesus' audience to be an outcast, goes out of his way to help the hurting man. The message of the parable is clear: Just because you say you do the work of God doesn't mean that you really do.

My imagination raises all kinds of questions about the motivation and circumstances of the priest, the Levite, and the Samaritan. What could have possibly been going on in the minds of the priest and the Levite that they could so easily have missed this opportunity to act as Jesus would want them to act? As an exercise, I'd like to approach the parable of the Good Samaritan in the spirit of Saint Ignatius of Loyola and his suggestion that we use our imagination to enter into the story and become part of the drama when reading the Bible. As the story unfolds we become an eyewitness. After taking a little poetic license with the story, I'm going to expound on the lessons we can learn from this rich and deeply affecting parable.

The Story as a Meditation

Eloy loved his life as a priest. He had wanted to be a priest all his life. He so loved God and the work in the Temple. He prided himself on the distinct way he dressed. Clothes make the man, and his vestments reminded people of how important he was. Eloy was a good singer of the Psalms. People told him that his teachings on God were profound. He was frequently asked to visit synagogues throughout the country to give inspiring talks.

One evening he was on his way to give a talk in Jericho. The synagogue leader said there would be at least three hundred men in attendance. Since women were segregated to another part of this holy place, this meant that at least another three hundred women would be listening from their place in the balcony. Jericho was one of the richest cities in Israel. When his boss, the high priest, heard that Eloy was going to Jericho he was delighted. "Make sure you take up a good collection," he said. "You know that we barely have enough to maintain this gigantic temple."

As he straightened his robe and the boxes with Scripture inside that were attached to his forehead and arm, he called out to his assistant, a Levite, "Jerrod, hurry up. We're going to be late."

"I'm going as fast as I can," Jerrod responded. "I've got to straighten out the scrolls the Pharisees used during a morning class. The floor is a mess. I'm going to be another thirty minutes. You go ahead and I'll catch up."

Eloy agreed but then had second thoughts. The road from Jerusalem to Jericho was a robber's paradise. It passed through hills, and thieves could strike and then easily escape. There would be more security if there were two of them traveling on the road. But he couldn't wait thirty minutes. Eloy couldn't be late because if he was he might not receive as much money from the people who were going to hear his talk. Besides, maybe with his fancy priest's robes, robbers wouldn't dare harm him. At least that was what he nervously muttered to himself as he set out on his journey.

Twenty minutes into the trip he came upon an ugly sight. Some poor man was on the side of the road naked and covered with blood. Eloy paused for only a moment. Oh, he knew what was going on. This was a decoy covered with red berry juice. If Eloy stopped the other robber would come rushing out and take his clothes and his possessions. Eloy rushed along. All this foolishness, he thought. He had more important things to do.

Ten minutes later Jerrod came running across the scene. He saw the ugly wounds on the man's head, side, and leg. He had taken a thorough beating. Should he stop? Oh, what a dilemma. He should help this poor man, but what about the talk in Jericho? If he wasn't around to organize the collection, Eloy would be furious. Jerrod might lose his job.

Then fortune smiled on him. Behind him was a man on a donkey. This man certainly didn't have Jerrod's pressing needs. Jerrod waved at the man and pointed to the unfortunate victim. When he felt sure the rider understood, he moved away toward Jericho at a brisk trot. He wouldn't be late.

The man on the donkey was a Samaritan. He stopped without hesitation to help the injured man. He brought him water, cleaned some of the blood with oil, poured wine into the man's wounds (which helped with the healing). Then he covered the man with his cloak. He helped him onto his donkey. He backtracked to an inn he had seen a couple miles before. There he rented a room. He spent the night comforting the wounded man through his fitful sleep. The next morning he left money with the innkeeper to cover the needs of the man. "If he needs anything, take care of it and I'll pay you when I return," he said. He headed back to Jerusalem, where he was sure he'd find a doctor.

The Samaritan was disappointed he was going to miss a visit with the family of a young girl he hoped to marry in Jericho. Since he missed his appointment, the family would probably reject him for being irresponsible. What a shame. But the Samaritan knew that by helping the injured man he was honoring God.

What I like about doing a meditative exercise like this is that it gives us perspective. We are no longer a person reading words, but a person *living* words. We become a pair of eyes in the story, and this gives us new insight.

Jesus uses the parable to show us the loving face of God. Unlike the officious priest and Levite who ignore the dying man, God is like the selfless Samaritan who sacrifices everything for us.

Our Call to Be the Samaritan

If we are to discover the loving face of God in this parable, we must act like the Samaritan. We are asked to put that face of God into action in our lives, to act like the giving Samaritan.

Ah, but that's more easily said than done. If we are honest with ourselves, how many of us would admit that we would choose to act like the priest and the Levite rather than the Samaritan? So what's the problem? One major difficulty is our confusion about what the Father considers "holy."

What Is Holy?

The two religious people in the story were considered holy because their whole lives were dedicated to a holy place: the Temple. They did holy things. The priest offered prayers and sacrifices to God. The Levite assisted the priest in serving God. In the eyes of those around them, both men were pretty devout people. And yet they didn't get it. Caught up in their service to God, they missed God's call in a big way. And what happened? A mere layman, a member of a heretical religious group for that matter, demonstrated the mercy that is at the center of the Father's heart.

Jesus turns our understanding of *holy* upside down. But before I say more, let's take a quick look at how we define the word *holy*.

Webster's New World Dictionary of American English defines *holy* as "Dedicated to religious use; belonging to or coming from God; consecrated; sacred. 2. Spiritually perfect or pure; untainted by evil or sin; saintly. 3. Regarded with or deserving deep respect, awe, reverence."

Yes, we can buy that. And if we wanted to use the word in context, we'd first say that God is holy. And then if we wanted to apply the term to a fellow human being we'd think of clergy or people who pray often and know the Bible. Yet sometimes "holy" people have a certain detached attitude when dealing with those who aren't part of the same group or religion. They can seem self-important and arrogant.

Our sense of holiness can, at times, be different from God's in many ways. The Father sees holiness in the face of those who care for the hurting. That can be uncomfortable news to many in the religious community who are not spending enough time with those who need help the most.

Yet who are the hurting? Surely, they are those people who are suffering through violence and poverty, those who are dying and are in need of emergency care. But the hurting are also people who are wounded by guilt and fear and depression and sin. They need to be cared for also. Many of us may never come upon a person dying in a ditch on the side of the road, but there are thousands, if not millions, of people we pass in the course of our life who could have used our assistance. Do we allow our prejudices to get in the way of our calling to serve those in need? Are we allowing the traditions of private or community prayer, days of worship, the demands of financing the building and maintaining of places of worship, intellectual pursuits, and the old need to have "time for ourselves" to get in the way of reaching out to our hurt, lost, and forgotten brothers and sisters?

I frequently hear people tell me that they couldn't go

to Communion, which is a very important part of being a Catholic. Recently, someone told me she had missed Sunday Mass because she had to stay home to care for a sick child, and she felt guilty about it. My response to her was, "Hurray for you. You saw the face of God in your child much more than many of the people who sat in the pews and had tuned God out." Don't let piety get in the way of holiness. That's the message at the center of the parable of the Good Samaritan.

That being said, we shouldn't make a case for *not going* to church because we are spending all our time caring for those in need. We can and must seek God's face in worship on a regular weekly basis. We must reverence holy places and people who give their life to worship and show us the importance of God in our lives. Still this experience of God in sacred places and with godly people should never exclude, as the parable reminds us, the call to serve those who are hurting.

Good Will, God's Will

In the Catholic Church we are aided in our understanding of holiness through the lives of the saints and the blessed. We are encouraged to study their lives and imitate them. Since we're assured that they're in heaven, we can confidently ask them to petition and pray to God for us and ask for his help in our needs.

One such saint was Peter Claver, a seventeenth-century

Jesuit who searched for the face of God on the crowded slave ships that docked in Cartagena, Colombia, after months on the sea, en route from Africa. Every month when the arrival of the slaves was signaled, Claver went out to meet them on the pilot's boat, carrying food and medicines. The slaves, cooped up in the hold, arrived crazed and brutalized by suffering and fear. Claver went to them, cared for them, showed them kindness, and made them understand that henceforth he was their defender and father. He thus won their goodwill by doing God's will.

One of the joys of my life was spending a few days with Mother Teresa and the Missionaries of Charity sisters in Mumbai and Calcutta, India. I saw firsthand the sisters' work of picking up the dead and dying from the streets. Mother's care for those who were hurting is a clear message to us of what holiness is.

The Desire to Be Elite

We live in a challenging world, one in which many people think they are better than others for various reasons. This prejudice arises in many of us because of feelings of inferiority or because cultural traditions have taught us that we are better than others. Many of us want to attain a certain level of elite status, whether it be with our looks or our intellect or our finances or even our spirituality— so that we might feel good about ourselves and overcome certain insecurities that seem to plague all of us. We feel better when we're admired. Yet, paradoxically, many of us secretly—and not so secretly—rejoice when people who think or act like they are better than us are brought down: politicians, religious, the rich, and celebrities. The way we are today really isn't much different from the way people were two thousand years ago, and the parable proves that. For Jesus' audience, the cultural understanding at the time was that priests were better than Levites, and both of them were better than the lowly, heretical Samaritans.

Yet Jesus turns the tables on this way of thinking. He makes the hero out of the outcast, the lesser person. From this parable our challenge is clear: We need to fight against putting one group of people above another. If we have the courage to follow the direction of the parable, the Father's love for us will be the strength we need to bridge the divide that separates many of us from experiencing the true glory of the Lord. As Pope John Paul II once said, we are all children of the same God.

Now we must act accordingly.

May "holiness" never hinder us from finding the face of God in the needy. And may we never consider ourselves so important and "elite"—like the priest and the Levite in the parable—that we miss God in those who are hurting around us.

Prayer for Reflection

Lord, thank you for the challenge of the parable. Help me find your face in the needy. Help me to always be open

*to those in need around me and to know that this care is
true holiness. Forgive me for struggling to be better than
others. With your love for me, let me relax and not be so
concerned with being more important than others.*

QUESTIONS FOR DISCUSSION

1. Who are today's Samaritans?
2. How do you define *holy*?
3. Who is holy in your eyes?
4. Are some people holier than others? How do you come to your conclusion?
5. What can you do to minister to the needy in your community or at your place of work?

7.

Poor

Matthew 25:31–40

"When the Son of Man comes in his glory, and all the angels with him, he will sit upon his glorious throne, and all the nations will be assembled before him. And he will separate them one from another, as a shepherd separates the sheep from the goats. He will place the sheep on his right and the goats on his left. Then the king will say to those on his right, 'Come, you who are blessed by my Father. Inherit the kingdom prepared for you from the foundation of the world. For I was hungry and you gave me food, I was thirsty and you gave me drink, a stranger and you welcomed me, naked and you clothed me, ill and you cared for me, in prison and you visited me.' Then the righteous will answer him and say, 'Lord, when did we see you hungry and feed you, or thirsty and give you drink? When did we see you a stranger and welcome you, or naked and clothe you? When did we see you ill or in prison, and visit you?' And the king will say to them in reply, 'Amen, I say to you, whatever you did for one of these least brothers of mine, you did for me.'"

Seeing God's Face in the Poor

The face of God that Jesus talks about in this parable is contained in the faces of the poor. This is a most challenging story because in some ways it's one of the most direct. Where is God? God is in the homeless, the wanderers looking for food, the ill who have no friends, strangers who feel ostracized and fearful, the prisoner serving time for committing a crime. We discover God's face breaking into our world in the embarrassed unemployed executive looking for a sandwich at a shelter, an alcoholic knocking at the door in the middle of the night asking for five dollars so he can get some gas to see his dying mother in Los Angeles, the lady with the nervous twitch on her face who is pushing us to move ahead as we stand in line at the Social Security office, the teenager with tattoos moaning in a corner as we wait our turn at the emergency room, as well as the wealthy lawyer who is crying over the loss of his wife and children through a divorce caused by his preoccupation with success and money.

All of these people and their circumstances may seem unrelated, but at the heart of each of their experiences is poverty, or a lack of something. Certainly, we look at the hungry, the thirsty, the strangers, the naked, the ill, and the imprisoned as the poor, but the poor that Jesus is talking about here is not a class of people. The poor can be found in every strata of life. The people who can't make mortgage payments and lose their homes are certainly poor, but many rich people who may have all the material gratifications one can imagine can experience the pangs of poverty. They are the spiritually poor, those who lack love in their lives or those who reject love for various reasons. Mother Teresa supported this idea as well in her book *No Greater Love*: "Often the rich are very spiritually poor people. I find it is easy to give a plate of rice to a hungry person, to furnish a bed to a person who has no bed, but to console or remove the bitterness, anger and loneliness that comes from being spiritually deprived, that takes a long time."

Then there are those between the rich and the very poor who, with a great deal of struggle, are just "making it." They too need to be served. The fact is, regardless of monetary wealth, each and every one of us can suffer from poverty: material poverty, poverty of spirit, poverty of faith, poverty of love, poverty of self-worth.

The parable's call to find God in the poor is a challenge that most of us are not naturally inclined to accept. We prefer the healthy to the sick and the secure to the destitute. We need God's help to move to a new orientation of our values. He has to give us new eyes to see and a new heart to feel. This happens through prayer and through God's gift of faith. It is this faith to believe in Jesus' words and accept the challenges that God sets forth in the Gospels that will lead us to see the fullness of God in the vacant areas of someone struggling to be filled.

Jesus Was Poor

This parable of Jesus is not an isolated call to give a priority to the poor. Even a cursory look at the Gospels shows that Jesus had a strong preference for the poor. In his view, the life of the wealthy was precarious. Jesus looked around and said to his disciples, "How hard it is for those who have wealth to enter the kingdom of God!" The disciples were amazed at his words. So Jesus again said to them in reply, "How hard it is for those who have wealth to enter the kingdom of God! . . . It is easier for a camel to pass through [the] eye of [a] needle than for one who is rich to enter the kingdom of God" (Mark 10:23, 25).

When a rich young man came to him with questions, Jesus challenged him:

> *"If you wish to be perfect, go, sell what you have and give to [the] poor, and you will have treasure in heaven. Then come, follow me." When the young man heard this statement, he went away sad, for he had many possessions. Then Jesus said to his disciples, "Amen, I say to you, it will be hard for one who is rich to enter the kingdom of heaven." (Matthew 19:21–23)*

He sent his disciples out to minister, advising them to take only the bare necessities:

*"He summoned the Twelve and began to send them
out two by two and gave them authority over unclean
spirits. He instructed them to take nothing for the
journey but a walking stick—no food, no sack, no
money in their belts. They were, however, to wear
sandals but not a second tunic." (Mark 6:7–9)*

Jesus was poor. He was born in a stable. He never had
a home to call his own. "Foxes have dens and birds of the
sky have nests, but the Son of Man has nowhere to rest his
head" (Luke 9:58). His public ministry with the apostles
and disciples was financed by the generosity of a group of
women from Galilee "who provided for them out of their
resources" (Luke 8:3).

When Jesus was seized by the Roman authorities, he
was beaten and jailed. At his death the only clothes he had
were taken by his executioners. He died naked.

Jesus may not have had much, but he had what mat-
tered most. He was filled with the Holy Spirit. The way Jesus lived his life and his call for his disciples to surrender to
his Father's care was radical, and his call for us today is to
let go of the preoccupation with getting more money than
we need for life's basics. As Jesus' disciples lost themselves
in sharing the Good News, their faith in God grew and they
confidently lived a life in which the Father took care of all
of their needs. And today we are called to confidently and
boldly live the same type of life.

The Richness of the Poor

Why did Jesus come down so strongly against the wealthy and take the side of the poor? For those who are willing to let go of undue material striving and put their faith in God's providential care, there are many possibilities of happiness.

The poor can have the richness of *being able to be close to God* because of their constant need of his help—be it food, shelter, clothing, education, or security. In their want, they are dependent on God for all things, and they are not distracted by the usual coveting that many of us experience today in society. In my own life I see this wealth of faith in Carmen, the young mother of three toddlers. Her husband has left her, she is unsure day to day if she will have a roof over her head or enough food for the children and herself. Yet she frequently comes to church to pray for an hour, and she does so intensely. She covers the enormity of her burdens with a gentle smile when she speaks to me, and a confident glance at the tabernacle in church as she prays amidst her restless children.

I see this faith in the tears and sometimes broken smiles of the women I minister to each month at the San Bernardino County Jail. Most are mothers who are longing for and praying for their children. Many of these ladies come from broken homes and abusive families. These are truly poor and damaged people, and many have surrendered their lives to the providence and care of the Father. Though dishonesty has landed many of them in jail, there is a richness in their honesty as prisoners, and I find much less hypocrisy in the county jail than on the streets.

When I visit the jail I go with two nuns from Mexico. We gather with the women in their dining hall. It's a cold, windowless room. While the Sister shares a biblical reflection in both English and Spanish, I move to a corner of the room. I sit at the metal bench and invite anyone who would like to come to talk, pray, or receive the Sacrament of Reconciliation. In many ways I'm a haven for these women. They know that I'll never tell the guards or the judge what they say. They have nothing to lose by being honest. They share their hearts and souls with me. Those who come are mostly sorry for what they have done. They long to be forgiven by the people they've hurt. They are fearful of returning to the seduction of drugs, prostitution, and running with the wrong people. Many have been forced to look at themselves with a candor they didn't have in their fast-paced and many times dangerous life outside prison. Many find a personal encounter with God through the Bible and the witnessing of other convicts. "When you get out, are you going to be able to turn your life around?" I ask them. Usually there is a pause as they reflect on how the wrong people have influenced their lives, plus the pull of drugs. A shy smile falls over many of their faces. "I hope I can, Father. Will you pray for me?"

I do, and I know that at that moment, people who were

empty, who were lacking so much, are filled with the loving grace of God the Father.

The poor can live with *deeper commitments to family*. Caesar and Irma, a poor couple in my congregation, suffered a terrible tragedy. Two months after Irma lost her mother, her father was visiting his wife's grave when a drug addict abducted him. Her father was forced to drive to an out-of-the-way spot in the mountains. He was stabbed to death and then his body was thrown down a hundred-foot-deep cavern. It took a week of frantic searching by family and police before the body was found. I remember the funeral Mass. The loving support of the family at this time of pain and sorrow showed me the presence of a deep and rich faith. Emotionally the family was overwhelmed with grief, and feelings of anger and revenge. This was deep poverty. I pointed to the imposing image of Jesus on the cross that hung over the altar. "Our faith tells us that God is with us at this moment," I said. "Look at the injustice. Look at the pain. Look at the death. There's no escaping the loss, the anger, the confusion, and the call for revenge. But we believe that Jesus overcame this tragedy with his resurrection. Your father shares this victory in heaven now. In the midst of all the violent emotions, rest a little in this love of Jesus for you. Hold on to your faith." As Irma and Caesar reached out and held each other and then embraced their children, I knew the power of family in the midst of tragedy.

Often I find the poor are rich in *generosity* as they share the little they have. They are able to give to others out of *what they need to live on* rather than giving from what they *don't need*. The collections at the four Masses we have each weekend are quite low. There are some who give larger donations, but the majority of the people give about a dollar a family. But then a special need arises—our two bathrooms need to be painted to cover the graffiti, or the roof on the reconciliation room needs to be replaced. Men and women are ready to give their time and talents to help. And then when we make an appeal for people suffering tragedies from earthquakes or floods in far-off countries, they reach deep into their pockets to help.

Jesus had an experience of the generosity of the poor. He was sitting in the Temple near the offering box and watching people put in their gifts. He noticed that many rich people were giving a lot of money. Finally, a poor widow came up and put in two coins that were worth only a few pennies. They were all she had to live on. Jesus told his disciples to gather around him. Then he said:

> *"Amen, I say to you, this poor widow put in more than all the other contributors to the treasury. For they have all contributed from their surplus wealth, but she, from her poverty, has contributed all she had, her whole livelihood." (Mark 12:43–44)*

Jesus' call to generosity also touched the wealthy tax collector Zacchaeus, who said, "Behold, half of my possessions, Lord, I shall give to the poor, and if I have extorted anything from anyone I shall repay it four times over" (Luke 19:8). Zacchaeus didn't give to the extent that the widow did, but this tax collector, a person ostracized from society in many ways like the Samaritan, certainly gave a lot.

The Evils of Poverty

Please don't get me wrong. I'm not trying to romanticize poverty. As I write this I know that because of poverty many people go through extreme suffering and hardship. Natural disasters, war, greed on the part of governments—all of this can bear down hard on God's people. Faithless, atheistic people cite many of these situations as evidence of the absence of God. Only with the gift of faith can our poverty bring blessings. With faith we believe that God loves us and will never let us down despite our poverty and need. And as people of faith it is our job to minister to others, to help build faith among the disenfranchised, to bring them to a new understanding of the world we all share. Though it's sometimes tough to grasp, we can be comforted again by Saint Paul's words as he cries out in the struggles of his own day and says, "We know that all things work for good for those who love God, who are called according to his purpose" (Romans 8:28).

Heroes Who Help the Poor

We all need heroes to help us aspire to the ideals Jesus is calling us to adhere to in the parable. In my work in the media I've had the privilege of traveling around the world and have visited many impoverished areas. I've been strongly moved by the courage and faith of people who have given up a lot to serve those in need. During my travels I visited a bombed-out building in Gaza. Through narrow passageways I entered the home of a Palestinian family. They offered me a cup of tea. A child showed me the bullet wounds in his leg. He explained that when he and his friends would gather together to protest, soldiers would shoot at their legs in an effort to discourage and frighten them. Later that day, in a graffiti-covered hospital, a doctor showed me a plastic cup filled with bullets extracted from young boys' legs. As we drove through a Gaza town, our car was pelted with stones thrown by some of those wounded and scarred boys. Our guide was a young Christian woman whose faith had compelled her to leave the States and serve the Palestinians through an international relief agency.

On another trip I spent some time in Mumbai, India, at a large factory building that had been donated to a community of nuns to care for handicapped children. I was shown around the facility by a young American tennis pro, who, with his wife and little daughter, had given up a year of their life on the tournament circuit to serve the children and thereby witness their faith in God. I remember entering a large converted warehouse room that was filled with little beds for handicapped kids. From the beds, two-hundred sets of dark eyes were silently questioning our entrance. The tennis pro stopped for a moment and then moved to a frail girl in a nearby bed. He picked her up by the waist and threw her high into the air and then caught her in his arms. The factory dormitory broke into loud squeals of laughter and chatter.

And then there was Manila. Like many cities in the developing world, this capital of the Philippines has a serious problem with the disposal of its garbage. One place used for that purpose is right by Manila Harbor, and it's called Smokey Mountain. The smoking garbage was piled about five stories high and spread over a square mile. There were 30,000 people living on or around Smokey Mountain. For six days I moved through the area with a television crew. Young and old roamed about with hooks and sacks, looking for any piece of metal or cardboard that could be sold. One young girl will forever be in my memory. There she was at her grungy, smelly work, hustling to get an early pick of the garbage as it was unloaded from a truck. She stood out because, along with her hook and sack, she wore a matching red cap, T-shirt, and boots. She was a poor, beautiful, and proud teenager. This is the parish of Father Ben. He's a Divine Word missionary who has been working with the people of Smokey Mountain for over thirty years. The stench of the toxic waste has damaged his lungs, but he continues to care for his people.

All these stories of the poor, and the heroes who serve

them, have inspired me to look for the face of God in everything and everyone. Each and every one of us is poor in some way, and that is what Jesus is calling us to be aware of in this parable. Be aware. Know that there is an emptiness in all of us and that we are called to fill it with the love of God the Father and the love of our neighbor.

How Can We Help the Poor?

As we consider the poor and our need to serve them, we face a bit of a dilemma. We can be overwhelmed by the number of poor who are near us and those around the world: the hungry, homeless, jobless, sick, uneducated, immigrants, prisoners, and refugees everywhere around us. Then there are those who seem to have everything who are suffering spiritual poverty. The enormity of the needs of the poor can leave us paralyzed.

If we turn to God in prayer, we will get some clarity as to how we can use our time, talent, and treasure to serve the poor. We can start by reaching out in a simple way to a needy person who is close to us, a stranger we meet in the bus station who asks for a dollar for a cup of coffee, a coworker who needs help with her electricity bill, a relative who needs a cosigner for a loan, a friend who needs some extra cash to buy a plane ticket for a parent's funeral, or a little girl in Latin America who can be helped by a pledge we make through a TV program. As we serve the poor, God bestows the grace of fulfillment. We are rewarded with a sense of purpose. We are serving not just our fellow person but, as the parable reminds us, God.

These glimpses into the sacredness of service may prompt us to take action so that the spirit of generosity will grow in us. Soon our desire to serve God in the poor we encounter may lead to the conviction that God will supply us with all the support we need as long as we are willing to give. As we give of ourselves, we can surrender all with the confidence that God will fill our empty baskets. Saint Paul spoke the blessings of generosity when he wrote:

> *Each must do as already determined, without sadness or*
> *compulsion, for God loves a cheerful giver. Moreover,*
> *God is able to make every grace abundant for you,*
> *so that in all things, always having all you need, you*
> *may have abundance for every good work. As it is*
> *written: "He scatters abroad, he gives to the poor; his*
> *righteousness endures forever." The one who supplies*
> *seed to the sower and bread for food will supply and*
> *multiply your seed and increase the harvest of your*
> *righteousness. (2 Corinthians 9:7–11)*

Prayer for Reflection

> *God, I need help to find Your Face in the poor—not*
> *only the homeless who are forced to sleep in doorways*
> *downtown, but in all people who suffer from emptiness*
> *of one form or another. May my faith in you move my*
> *eyes, my hands, and my feet. Help me to give back to*

you the gifts you have given to me by being generous to others.

QUESTIONS FOR DISCUSSION

1. What does it mean to be spiritually poor?
2. How do you deal with the media's overwhelming images of the poor and the suffering, and the appeals for help that you receive from the media?
3. Can you relate a "high" you had when you were especially generous?
4. How can you find God in someone who repulses you?

8.

Forgiving

Luke 7:36–48

A Pharisee invited him to dine with him, and he entered the Pharisee's house and reclined at table. Now there was a sinful woman in the city who learned that he was at table in the house of the Pharisee. Bringing an alabaster flask of ointment, she stood behind him at his feet weeping and began to bathe his feet with her tears. Then she wiped them with her hair, kissed them, and anointed them with the ointment.

When the Pharisee who had invited him saw this he said to himself, "If this man were a prophet, he would know who and what sort of woman this is who is touching him, that she is a sinner." Jesus said to him in reply, "Simon, I have something to say to you." "Tell me, teacher," he said. "Two people were in debt to a certain creditor; one owed five hundred days' wages and the other owed fifty. Since they were unable to repay the debt, he forgave it for both. Which of them will love him more?" Simon said in reply, "The one, I suppose, whose larger debt was forgiven." He said to him, "You have judged rightly."

Then he turned to the woman and said to Simon, "Do you see this woman? When I entered your house, you did not give me water for my feet, but she has bathed them with her tears and wiped them with her hair. You did not give me a kiss, but she has not ceased kissing my feet since the time I entered. You did not anoint my head with oil, but she anointed my feet with ointment. So I tell you, her many sins have been forgiven; hence, she has shown great love. But the one to whom little is forgiven, loves little." He said to her, "Your sins are forgiven."

A Tender Story

One of Jesus' chief teachings is that God the Father is a forgiving God. This is most apparent in this parable, one of my favorites.

Imagine you were standing at the door of Simon's home watching this incident. Jesus is reclining on a cushion with the others around him in a semicircle. In the middle of them is the food, and all the diners are eating without utensils. A woman enters the scene. We don't know what sin, or sins, she has committed to be labeled "a sinner," but her status as an outsider is clear for all to see. Many have speculated that she was a prostitute, since this would explain how her sins were known to the town. Though no words are reported as being spoken between Jesus and the woman, we can imagine that there is a silent exchange that pierces her most intimately. Maybe it is an unspoken prayer Jesus prays asking for the Holy Spirit to help her change her life. He certainly doesn't call her a terrible person. He doesn't judge her. His respect and love for her stir in her conscience.

And how does she express her thanks? In the best way she knows: with a public expression of service and reverence. She courageously enters the dining room, falls at Jesus' feet, sobs, anoints his feet with oil, and then dries them with her hair. And what happens? Jesus accepts her emotionally charged expression of devotion, although to those who are gathered there in the home of a Pharisee what she does seems scandalous. In the process, Christ reveals the open and forgiving face of God to the woman, to the Pharisee, to his apostles, and to us.

Forgiveness. For many of us this is a very difficult topic, because even though we've been taught that God is a loving God, do we believe that God really is a forgiving God? Many of us have serious misgivings that God would forgive us for the horrible things we've done in the past, let alone the heinous crimes of thieves, rapists, and murderers.

Why do we think this way? Maybe it has something to do with our difficulty in forgiving others. It's tough for many of us to excuse others for the things they have done, so we think it must be tough for God to forgive us. But our ways are not God's ways. God is not going to be outdone by our expectations that God sets limits on his forgiveness. Moreover, God the Father's forgiveness can be found all through the Gospels. We see the Father's loving forgiveness in the story of the sinful woman. There is the story of the prodigal son, which brings our idea of God's capacity to forgive to new levels. Then there is the episode of the religious leaders who wanted to stone a woman caught in the act of adultery. Jesus offered her forgiveness as the accusers walked away, unwilling to cast the first stone. At the Last Supper Jesus says, "This is the cup of my blood, the blood of the new and everlasting covenant. It will be shed for you and for all so that sins may be forgiven." And ultimately, hanging from the cross, Jesus pleads with God to exonerate his persecutors: "Father, forgive them."

The Burden of Not Forgiving Others

Yet even though Jesus has shown us the way, our spiritual GPS can malfunction and many of us frequently have a tough time forgiving others—both those who hurt us personally and all those people who do terrible things to others. We want to condemn to the depths of hell those who abuse children or those men who abandon their wives, leaving them to raise a family alone. We have a natural inclination to want to call for the death penalty for terrorists and war criminals.

We can become enslaved by this refusal to forgive. As we stubbornly carry around this belief that we have been wronged, it quickly becomes a heavy burden that drags us down and has a deadening effect on our soul.

Case in point, some years ago I was attending a meeting with other priests. I was anxious to tell them of the work that I was doing with television in order to get their support for my ministry. To my surprise a priest began criticizing me at length. To this day I don't understand the reason for his vitriol, but regardless, I was embarrassed, humiliated, and angry! Although some of the things he said were true, I was so caught up in my irritation with this man that I wasn't able to respond. After the meeting I went back to my job. Outwardly I seemed unfazed by his actions, but for a long time I bore the burden of not forgiving him. I frequently recalled the situation and his words, and my soul grew heavy because I was not able to forgive him. In time, though, I came to the awareness that I was hurting myself by having an unforgiving attitude. Nevertheless, even though I was still angry, whenever his name came up I tried to speak positively of him to others. With great difficulty I prayed that God would bless him. Secretly I bore this pain for fifteen years. Then just this year I had a chance meeting with him. He was celebrating a Mass I attended. I went into the sacristy to say hello while he was dressing for Mass. I greeted him with warmth and a big smile. I truly admired him and the creative work he was doing in his ministry. He looked at me with a quiet smile. "Mike, it's good to see you." We shook hands.

I responded, "It's been a long time. How are you doing?"

"Oh, I'm getting older, but I'm still plugging away." I took my seat in the church. When he came out to say Mass he acknowledged me to the community and praised me for my perseverance in working in the difficult field of media. After Mass we shared breakfast and talked of the good old times. We left each other with an embrace. And at that moment, either because of mature communication or because of all my prayers over the years (either way it doesn't matter, it was all grace from God) our reconciliation lifted a heavy burden from my heart. With our coming together I experienced the Father's forgiveness.

Forgiveness Is a Process

Occasionally we have been so hurt that we believe that we cannot forgive another person. Forgiveness is not possible. The desire to forgive takes a back seat to desires for anger and vengeance. We want the person who has hurt us to feel pain. God can forgive because he's God. For us, it's not so easy.

The only way to crack the impossibility of forgiving is to turn to God for help. We must ask him to give us the smallest stirring of a desire to forgive. Asking God for this help is a monumental decision. After we have put our challenge in God's hands we must surrender to the belief that God will answer our prayer.

Forgiving others is difficult, but it is helpful to remember that forgiving takes time. Certainly, forgiveness can happen in a simple and complete way. I turn to the person who has hurt me and say, "I forgive you." The process is finished. We are both able to move ahead with a clean slate. Yes, forgiveness can happen like that and has many times in my life.

But sometimes forgiveness can be a long, painful process. It's like a wound that takes days or weeks or months to heal. Once a bone is broken, it needs time to mend, right? And that is what is at the center of forgiveness—healing. Forgiveness is a healing process, and all the struggles that take place—whether it is fear of something happening again or facing problems with a lack of confidence—are steps on a journey that will ultimately lead you to the loving face of the Father.

Can We Forgive Ourselves?

As we've discussed, even though Jesus was good at it, forgiving is a difficult task, and sometimes the most difficult person to forgive is ourself. After committing what we consider a serious sin, sometimes the memory of what we have done can linger in our conscience with feelings of guilt all our lives. Even if we've whispered regret to the person we've hurt, even if we've asked God's forgiveness, even if we have mustered up the courage to speak our sin in the Sacrament of Reconciliation, many of us will doubt that God will forgive us. We feel unworthy of forgiveness because we believe we're guilty. We may be responsible for damaging our life or the lives of those we profess to love. That sense of obsessive regret can separate us from God.

Despite these negative attitudes, we must be willing to forgive ourselves, to believe in God's love for us and his desire to forgive us. God knows that when we become overwhelmed by our wrongdoing, we stifle the creative freedom he wants us to manifest. He knows that when we're in the prison of doubting his forgiveness, we're failing to fulfill his dream, we're not playing the vital part we're meant to play in ushering his Kingdom into the world. Our faith in God's love can become the foundation for beginning to forgive ourselves. When we forgive ourselves, we are free to use our talents to help others. We are free to change our lives. We are free to love.

As a priest, I see the common struggle to accept God's forgiveness when people confess over and over sins they committed many years ago. They mention the sin again— "just to be sure I'm forgiven." This inability to accept God's forgiveness is a serious failure to accept God's love. But how do we forgive ourselves? How do we let go of past sins?

There is no fixed formula, but prayer is a good starting point. Pray to God for the grace to understand and accept his forgiveness, and then take action and make it a point to forgive anyone who asks forgiveness of you. Forgiving others helps us find the face of the Father in ourselves.

You may be saying, "Thanks, but what else have you got?" Well, here's another idea, and you might reject my suggestion because in some ways it seems a little dishonest, but I believe it can be a great step in finding the long sought after forgiveness of past sins, especially when forgiving yourself seems like an impossibility. Here it goes. It's radical. I've warned you.

Just act as if you believe in complete forgiveness—even if you don't!

On the intellectual level you know you are forgiven. The Gospels tell us so. But the emotional acceptance of this truth may elude you. You wish you could have the freedom and peace you see in others who have sinned but have been able to move on with their lives with confidence in the Father's forgiveness. Study those people you admire. Then adapt what you see in your own life and act as if it were true, because it is!

Embrace the joy of forgiveness. Accept the freedom of forgiveness. Act like you're the most fortunate person in the world. You have a Father God who has embraced you, and you can dance with him in a new confidence. Become an actor assuming a new character. You know the script from the stories of the Bible. Become the woman washing Jesus' feet. Hear his words of forgiveness and walk out a new person. You will be surprised, because before you know it you will feel the truth of God's forgiveness, because you will have lived it.

Forgive God?

Forgiving others and forgiving ourselves can be difficult, but sometimes forgiving God can be the most difficult thing we'll ever have to do. Although this might sound blasphemous, we must face the reality that sometimes we are angry with God. We may see him as responsible for the dysfunctional family we were raised in. We may see him as responsible for the cancer that attacks the people we love. God can sometimes seem like the source of the power struggles and abuses we experience in the Church. Where is God when a couple loses an infant? Why does he allow the parents of seven young children to divorce? Sometimes we hold a grudge against God for not stepping in and making things better, and this grudge can make us angry and frustrated. Sometimes, when we are hurt and angry, the last thing in the world we want to do is forgive anyone, let alone God.

Yet the Bible can help us deal with these dark feelings. As a young boy Jeremiah was called to be a prophet. During his life he suffered a lot. He lived in Jerusalem at the time the Babylonians held the city in the clutches of a siege. God told Jeremiah to go to the king and the leaders of the people and tell them to surrender. This message did not go over well. The prophet was scorned by the leadership. At one point he was placed in stocks and exposed to the ire of the whole city. Later he was thrown down a well and left to die. Some friends pulled him out. All of this suffering prompted him to come out with one of the more shocking statements in the Bible. The angry Jeremiah looked to God and cried, "You duped me, O LORD, and I let myself be duped; you were too strong for me, and you triumphed. All the day I am an object of laughter; everyone mocks me" (Jeremiah 20:7).

God did not come crashing down on Jeremiah for his impudence. His anger with God was honest and accepted by God.

We who fester in anger with God and struggle with not wanting to forgive him need to confidently express our feelings to God and know that God is big enough to accept our anger. This freedom to express our anger is part of the process of healing and growing in intimacy with God. "God, help me to understand you. Help me to forgive you." Only with this honesty will we be free. Only by forgiving God can we begin to develop a loving, intimate relationship with him.

Forgiveness: God's Plan to Change the World

God has a definite plan in calling us to forgiveness. In his battle to overcome sin he wants us to use forgiveness rather than vengeance. He wants the world to work together for unity, which affirms life—and God. Look at the violence on display in the newspapers and on TV. If gang members knew how to forgive, we wouldn't have drive-by shootings. If terrorists knew how to forgive and work for justice, suicide bombings would end. Forgiveness is the way of bridging whatever gulf separates people. To forgive is to begin to heal the fracturedness that seems to be tearing our world apart.

Forgive and Forget

We have heard the statement "I can forgive, but I can't forget." Forgiving another might be possible, but we may still carry the memory of the pain inflicted on us. We sometimes can't let go. Unfortunately we tend to project onto God our need to hold on to hurtful memories. If we can't forget, then it seems reasonable to believe that God can't forget either. Oh, but when we truly look at the face of God that Jesus talks about in the parable of the sinful woman, we see something very different. Christ doesn't harp on the past. All that matters is the present, and what's even more encouraging is that there are plenty of places in Scripture where God says that he not only forgives us but forgets our sins as well:

It is I, I, who wipe out, for my own sake, your offenses; your sins I remember no more. (Isaiah 43:25)

Lo, I am about to create new heavens and a new earth; the things of the past shall not be remembered or come to mind. (Isaiah 65:17)

[F]or I will forgive their evildoing and remember their sin no more. (Jeremiah 31:34)

But, to be perfectly fair, there is this line from the Book of Revelation that seems to say something different. It paints an image of God writing down and remembering all the bad things we've done:

"I saw the dead, the great and the lowly, standing before the throne, and scrolls were opened. Then another scroll was opened, the book of life. The dead were judged according to their deeds, by what was written in the scrolls." (Revelation 20:12)

How do we reconcile the two images of God in the Bible? One God forgets my sins and the other writes down my offenses to make sure I'm accountable. When I face these seeming contradictions in the Bible I must concede that both are true. God, through the love of his Son Jesus Christ, wipes my slate clean, but that doesn't mean my actions haven't been duly noted. When I have to choose one God or the other, I choose the more loving and gracious God as ultimately more important, while acknowledging that the scorekeeper God uses my awareness of my misdeeds as a means to draw me closer to him in love. After reading Isaiah I have another image: I am coming up to the gates of heaven and God is frantically searching for those notes on my life. Finally he turns to me and says in frustration and embarrassment, "Oh, I can't remember where I put those notes. You know me and my bad memory. Come on in!"

Forgive but Set Boundaries

Jesus teaches us to turn the other cheek, give your shirt too when asked for your coat, go two miles when forced to go one, lend without expecting a return, forgive not seven but seventy times seven times.

These teachings can leave the impression that imposed limits are not part of the Father's plan. Yet we know that setting limits is a vital part of growing. A child needs limits, so a parent will pick him up and carry him away from danger. A teenager needs time boundaries imposed by his parents to balance study and recreation. When people are ruining their lives and the lives of others with drugs, we need police to restrain and confine them. On a larger scale, we need an army to keep us safe from peoples and nations that war against us.

The commandments are God's way of establishing limits to our freedom. The commandments lay the pattern for living in community in peace and security. If we love God and love our neighbor as ourselves, we will discipline children, restrain criminals, and go to war to defend our country if it is being oppressed and endangered.

But then what about turning the other cheek and so forth? To make sense of this question, I turn to the wisdom of Ecclesiastes and the statement that there's a time for everything (Ecclesiastes 3). There's a time when injustice against one person wakes us up to the injustice being perpetrated against the many. And there's a time when being hit by an abusive husband requires fleeing the house and calling the cops. There's a time to forgive a grown daughter who has stolen your life savings, and there's a time to tell her she can no longer live under your roof because of the scandal she causes to your other children by her use of alcohol. Yet, even when circumstances force us to set limits, we must remember that these limits apply only to actions and never to people. We keep ourselves safe, but beyond this we imitate Jesus and forgive. And we never write any person off as beyond reach.

The Joy of Being Forgiven

The face of the forgiving Father is at the heart of the joy and happiness we seek in life. When we run from forgiving ourselves and others, we can wallow in fear, anxiety, anger, guilt, and even depression. Yet, when we pray and through the grace of God we become aware of the Father's forgiveness, and when this faith in his love allows us to muster the courage to forgive ourselves or say "I'm sorry" to another—when we do this we touch on life's deepest and richest joy. We understand ourselves better. We know the other person intimately. And we know more profoundly the face of the forgiving Father.

Prayer for Reflection

> *God, I believe that you forgive me like Jesus forgave and accepted the woman in the parable. Thank you. Help me to honor your forgiveness by forgiving myself and others. Also God there are times when I'm angry and upset with you. I ask you for your grace to help me journey down the road to forgiveness in my relationship with you. Thank you for your love. Thank you for the joy of your forgiveness.*

QUESTIONS FOR DISCUSSION

1. What are some of the things we can do to help overcome the guilt of past sins?

2. What happens when we forgive others?
3. Are there some people who don't deserve to be forgiven? Explain your answer and use it as a means for entering into a prayerful dialogue with God.
4. Have you struggled to forgive God? Describe your experience.

9.

Authentic

Luke 18:10–14

"Two people went up to the temple area to pray; one was a Pharisee and the other was a tax collector. The Pharisee took up his position and spoke this prayer to himself, 'O God, I thank you that I am not like the rest of humanity—greedy, dishonest, adulterous—or even like this tax collector. I fast twice a week, and I pay tithes on my whole income.'

"But the tax collector stood off at a distance and would not even raise his eyes to heaven but beat his breast and prayed, 'O God, be merciful to me a sinner.'

"I tell you, the latter went home justified, not the former; for everyone who exalts himself will be humbled, and the one who humbles himself will be exalted."

Wait a Minute!

Now let me get this straight. God the Father is pleased with sinners? You mean to tell me that the religious man, the Pharisee who's doing all the right things, wasn't pleasing to God? The one who talks to God graciously, the one who's not greedy but generous, the one who's honest and not deceitful, the one who's faithful to his wife, the one who fasts in the name of God, the one who tithes? That guy? If someone had passed this man's résumé on to me as a pastor, I'd throw out a red carpet and welcome him to my parish. What an example he would be to the other parishioners. Not to mention that 10 percent of what he earns he's going to give to the Church.

Yet, even though the Pharisee seems to be doing all the right things, God the Father is more pleased with a disreputable tax collector. Come on! Nobody likes tax collectors! In Jesus' time they were disliked for several reasons. In the first century A.D., Palestine had been occupied by the Romans and their military for almost a hundred years. To understand how the people of Palestine felt, try to imagine what it would be like for us to have lost one of our wars and have the enemy come in with troops and rulers and tell us how to live. We would chafe strongly against strangers controlling us and demanding that we pay taxes that would go to the maintenance of the occupying force and the pockets of rulers in a far-off country. The tax collectors in Jesus' time were natives of the land who were collaborating with the occupying force.

The Romans sold the right to collect taxes to the highest bidder. Once the collector paid his allotment to the Romans, he could keep everything else. For this reason, tax collectors were notoriously dishonest. They were called "publicans" because they were collectors of public revenue, revenue for the hated Romans. Having contact with the

Romans made tax collectors ritually unclean in the eyes of the Jewish citizens. They were numbered with the "unreligious" outcasts of society. It is no surprise that in the New Testament they are linked with prostitutes and "sinners." They were considered traitors and apostates.

I'm sure that as Jesus was telling this story, the listeners were gulping in disbelief that he would weave a tale that made a hated tax collector look good, and, what's more, say that God was pleased with him. Jesus wanted to make a strong point about who is pleasing to his Father. The story shows a flash of his strong courage.

What is the face of the Father we see in this parable? God is pleased with people who sin and then repent. The Father is pleased with the tax collector and us when we honestly face our sin and repent. He's more pleased with a repentant sinner than with the highfalutin religious person who can list his virtues and sacrifices to show his love of God. The repentant tax collector is authentic.

The Story as a Meditation

Let's once again employ the prayer method of Saint Ignatius, who invites us to use our imagination to help us meditate on the parables. Let's come up with possible circumstances that pushed this hated man of the people to come to God with the conviction of his sin. What was the sin that pushed him to repentance and thus made him so pleasing to the Father?

Imagine that our tax collector is visiting the home of a man who has fallen behind in his payments. We'll call the tax collector Harold and the man he's visiting Frederick.

"Frederick, this is the third time that I've visited you," says the tax collector. "You know you have not paid your taxes."

"I know, Harold. I have fallen on some tough times," Frederick responds. "I got laid off from my job last month. I've had to dip into the little savings I have to feed my family. Then my little two-year-old daughter came down with a cough. I've had to go to the doctor and get medicine. Please, can you give me more time to pay?"

"You have to realize I hear hard stories like this all the time," Harold says. "I have a boss who puts pressure on me to collect the payments. If I don't get the money, I'll get fired and lose all that I've worked for."

"Please, come in," Frederick says. "Let me show you my daughter. Once you've seen her I know you'll understand. If I give you the tax money, I won't be able to take care of her."

"No. I've got my duty to do," Harold says dismissively. "Give me the money or I'll have my people come and throw you and your family out in the street."

Frederick goes back into the house and comes out with the tax money. He says nothing as Harold snatches up the coins and leaves.

One month later, Harold comes knocking at Frederick's door. It's time for the monthly tax payment. After Frederick opens the door he says nothing but turns to go back inside. Harold thinks he's going to get the money. When

Frederick reappears at the door he doesn't have money in his hands; instead he carries the lifeless body of his two-year-old daughter. Harold looks at the dead girl for only a moment and then turns with a scream and runs to the Temple, where Jesus' parable begins.

How do you think the tax collector felt? I'm sure not many of us would sympathize with him, but the guilt must have been horrendous. It is in this darkness, in the realization of his actions, that the tax collector drops to his knees and begs God's forgiveness. The tax collector is authentic. He pleases God because he honestly faces his sin and turns to God for mercy.

The apostle Paul typifies for us this honest surrender to the truth of our sinfulness:

> *For I know that good does not dwell in me, that is, in my flesh. The willing is ready at hand, but doing the good is not. For I do not do the good I want, but I do the evil I do not want. Now if [I] do what I do not want, it is no longer I who do it, but sin that dwells in me. (Romans 7:18–20)*

When we face our weaknesses and our sinfulness, we are pleasing to God. God accepts us in our brokenness, and this is a cause for celebration. Paul continues in another letter:

> *[B]ut [God] said to me, "My grace is sufficient for you, for power is made perfect in weakness." I will rather*

*boast most gladly of my weaknesses, in order that
the power of Christ may dwell with me. Therefore,
I am content with weaknesses, insults, hardships,
persecutions, and constraints, for the sake of Christ;
for when I am weak, then I am strong.* (2 Corinthians
12:9–10)

Yes, when we are weak, we are strong.

Facing Our Sins—the Good Versus the Better

Often our main problem with facing sin in our lives is our obsession with justifying our actions. We are ready to prove to ourselves and everyone else that we are doing something good. Take, for example, a young lady who is facing a difficult decision. Let's call her Brittany. She wants to move in with her boyfriend and become sexually active with him outside of marriage. On one side her parents are telling her not to do this. Two of the girl's best friends tell her not to do it. Sister Maureen and Father Phil from her parish tell her it would be a bad move. But Brittany still wants to live with her boyfriend.

How does she justify what her family, friends, and members of her church tell her is a sin? Where will she find a "good" to justify shacking up with her boyfriend? She equates the "good" in her decision with the sweeping virtues of freedom and love. Brittany knows her Bible: "Didn't

Jesus say, 'The truth will set you free'? The truth is I love my boyfriend. Jesus is on my side. And doesn't Saint Paul himself say that we should be free from the law? And as for love, doesn't the first letter of John say that God is love? 'Beloved, let us love one another, because love is of God; everyone who loves is begotten by God and knows God. Whoever is without love does not know God, for God is love'" (1 John 4:7–8).

"I choose that freedom," Brittany says. "I choose love. Don't you understand that what I'm doing is good?" And so she moves in with her boyfriend. She denies the wisdom of those who love her and chooses what she sees as the lofty values of freedom and love.

The example shows the need we have in every decision always to search out a good. The problem is that sometimes we choose the wrong good—a course of action that merely seems to be good.

When we have a choice between goods, our goal in life is to choose the better, or the best when there are many options. The saying is true: "The road to hell is paved with good intentions." The truth of life is that we will find a good in anything we want. The call of living a moral life is finding and choosing *the better*. And how do we know *the better*? Again, we turn to the commandments. It's better to honor our parents rather than curse them even though we may disagree with them. It's better to be faithful to my wife rather than commit adultery even though she's more occupied with the children and her work than she is with me. It's better not to steal a car even though I know I'll have a thrill in driving it.

Jesus pushes the challenge of choosing *the better* when he says that it's better to turn the other cheek rather than seek vengeance for the death of a family member. It's better to love our enemies and do good to those who persecute us, even when the prospect of striking back at them seems so satisfying.

The tax collector in our imagined version of the parable chose the good of his job over the obligations of God's law. He had to demand the tax money because he didn't want to lose his job—because that would not be good. Then how would he feed his family? But then the moment of grace came. In our imagined scenario, he saw the body of the dead two-year-old girl. He had contributed to her death. In an instant he saw his sin and faced the truth before God.

We, too, are challenged to face our sins. Are we doing good in our lives? I'm sure we are. The challenge of the parable is to stop and ask ourselves if we are willing to embrace the better, and the best.

The Sin of the Pharisee— "I'm Better Than You Are"

Now that we've looked at the tax collector, let's shift our focus to the other character in the parable. What is the sin of the Pharisee? In short, he thinks he's better than the tax collector. Let's call it the "I'm better than you are" sin.

Jesus railed against this type of sin, as we can see in the Gospels. There is the story in which Jesus speaks with, and shows love to, the sinful Samaritan woman at the well. Not only does he talk with a hated Roman centurion, a leader in the Roman army, but he is willing to go to the man's house to cure his servant. And then there is the time when Christ is walking ahead of his disciples on their way to the town of Capernaum. The apostles think Jesus isn't listening to their conversation. He is. When they arrive at their destination, he asks them, "What were you arguing about along the way?" They had been arguing about which one of them was the greatest, and so they do not answer. After Jesus sits down and tells the twelve apostles to gather around him, he says, "If anyone wishes to be first, he shall be the last of all and the servant of all" (Mark 9:33–34). With this story Jesus takes the air out of the apostles' drive to be one up on their fellow apostles.

This brings us back to the parable of the Pharisee and the tax collector. Jesus is reconfirming that God the Father loves all people and is most happy when one of his people repents and acknowledges his sinfulness.

Why is this "I'm better than you are" attitude so serious? Because this approach to life leads to serious division in our world. For a man to say to a woman that he's better than she is opens the door to oppression and conflict. When one nation says to another that we're better than you, the nation being put down will try to prove the other wrong and this can lead to violence, terrorism, and war. Perhaps one of the most destructive uses of the "I'm better than you are" attitude comes when one religion says it's better than another: "I've got the truth of God and you don't." All too often the result is persecution and the destruction of God's creation.

Letting Go of "I'm Better Than You Are"

Letting go of the attitude of superiority can be difficult. As Christians we believe that we are loved by God. Paul said that we have become adopted members of God's family and that we have a special relationship with the Father. Given that blessing, it seems quite natural for us to feel superior to those who don't enjoy this intimacy.

Yet we should never be so wrapped up in our intimacy with God that we forget the importance of not judging others. Yes, the Father loves us and we should revel in our intimacy with him, but God's love is big enough for all his creations. We don't have to compare ourselves to others. Rather than treat others as inferior, we should search out evidence of God's love for them and enrich our relationship with the Father through them. Here are just a few things we can learn from other religions that can enhance our lives in rich and beautiful ways:

- The Jewish people have deep reverence for the Bible. As Catholics and Christians we can learn from this example to study the Scriptures in more detail and increase our respect for the holy word of God.

- Many Muslim women highlight modesty in their dress. This is a reminder to us to be more modest in our way of living. Muslims also pray five times a day, and we can learn from their faithfulness the need to make special time each day to enter into conversation and adoration with Jesus and God the Father.
- Many Mormons dedicate two years of their life to missionary work. Let us learn from them to awaken to the call to share our faith with others.
- Some nondenominational churches are attracting large numbers of Catholics. We need to study how these churches appeal to people by how they teach and how they serve their flock so that we might learn how to minister to the needs of people before they leave our congregations.

The parable we have been studying in this chapter calls us to stop looking down on others as inferior. The solution is to act like the tax collector in the story. We must face our sin and humbly go to God begging his mercy and forgiveness. The fruits of this type of surrender are that we can then experience God's love and know that we are accepted in God's eye. With the grace of this awareness we don't have to try to prove to others that we're better than they are. As we accept the truth that God is pleased with us we can have enough security to now see how God loves others. We can even delight in the blessings God has given others. We can empower them and be enriched in our relationship with the Father through them.

Prayer for Reflection

God give me the courage to face the sin in my life. Next, lead me into repentance. Let me relax in your love for all people. Little by little help me to let go of the drive to prove I'm better than others. Let your personal love for me be my security, my peace.

QUESTIONS FOR DISCUSSION

1. What can you do to be humble with God?
2. When was the last time you worked on changing a habit? Did it work for you?
3. What are some of the "good" things that you're doing that you could do "better"?
4. What truths can you learn from other religions? Identify two or three things from another faith-based community that can help you serve God better, and put those into action.

10.

Generous

Matthew 20:1–16

"The kingdom of heaven is like a landowner who went out at dawn to hire laborers for his vineyard. After agreeing with them for the usual daily wage, he sent them into his vineyard. Going out about nine o'clock, he saw others standing idle in the marketplace, and he said to them, 'You too go into my vineyard, and I will give you what is just.' So they went off. (And) he went out again around noon, and around three o'clock, and did likewise. Going out about five o'clock, he found others standing around, and said to them, 'Why do you stand here idle all day?'

"They answered, 'Because no one has hired us.' He said to them, 'You too go into my vineyard.'

"When it was evening the owner of the vineyard said to his foreman, 'Summon the laborers and give them their pay, beginning with the last and ending with the first.' When those who had started about five o'clock came, each received the usual daily wage. So when the first came, they thought that they would receive more, but each of them also got the usual wage. And on receiving it they grumbled against the landowner, saying, 'These last ones worked only one hour, and you have made them equal to us, who bore the day's burden and the heat.'

"He said to one of them in reply, 'My friend, I am not cheating you. Did you not agree with me for the usual daily wage? Take what is yours and go. What if I wish to give this last one the same as you? Or am I not free to do as I wish with my own money? Are you envious because I am generous?'

"Thus, the last will be first, and the first will be last."

Is God Fair?

My aunt and godmother Hazel was a wonderful Christian. She attended church every Sunday and sometimes during the week too. I remember one morning when I was still in grade school, as we drove home from church, she commented on the Gospel story of the workers in the vineyard that we had heard at Mass. She said, "It's not fair. Some terrible sinner lives his whole life enjoying all those sins and then on his deathbed repents and can get into heaven scot-free. And here I am trying to be faithful all my life and I get the same reward? I can't accept that. It's not fair." I was in no position to contradict the mighty Aunt Hazel. For that matter, what would I say? What she said made a lot of sense. I have always struggled with this parable too. I remember I smiled at her and kept my mouth shut.

Now that she's passed on, I can muster the courage

to respond to her. Aunt Hazel, you were right. The employer's actions do seem unjust by our standards. Can you imagine the war that would break out if a parent gave the same reward to a child who had worked all day at painting the house as to a child who had merely come along at the end of the work to put the finishing touches on the job? The cry of "injustice" would be loud and clear. It's like the faithful son becoming indignant when the father killed the fatted calf for his prodigal, derelict son. Many of us still have a problem with that story as well.

The only answer I can come up with is that the God of the workers in the vineyard parable is different from me. Much different. And the principles and values that many of us hold dear are still far different from the great Almighty's standards. The word *magnanimous* comes to mind. A big word. It comes from the Latin for a "great soul." For me that means God loves me in a way that is deeper and richer than I could ever comprehend. Even if I'm a sinner, he loves me. Even if I fail in fulfilling the dreams he has put in my heart, he loves me. Even if I'm lazy, he keeps prodding me with his love. Even if I'm convinced that there's no hope for me, he loves me. With God there is always hope. With God, it's never too late to ask for forgiveness.

Letting Go of Trying to Prove
My Worth Before God

Nevertheless, there's something more about the image of God we find in the parable. We can be sure God is pleased when we follow his commandments and inspirations. The important question is our motivation. Why do we go to church? Why do we pray? Why do we try to keep away from off-color jokes? Why don't we rob banks? Why do we try to avoid scandalizing people? Are we acting out of pride, hoping that we'll be seen and admired by others? Are we driven by fear of being punished? Are we motivated by trying to earn God's love and salvation?

From this "workers" parable I can learn to relax with the assurance that there isn't anything that I can do to make God love me. Saint Paul struggled with people who put undue importance on fulfilling the law. He was especially concerned with the law of circumcision. Without true faith in God, complying with the law meant nothing. In his letter to the Romans Paul wrote, "What occasion is there then for boasting? It is ruled out. On what principle, that of works? No, rather on the principle of faith. For we consider that a person is justified by faith apart from works of the law" (Romans 3:27–28). God loves us even before we lift a finger. He loves us unconditionally. He loves us more than we can imagine. He loves us more than all the great acts we do to prove our love. Ah, the peace this belief brings! The security. We can rest in the arms of a God who loves us just as we are merely by having faith in his love.

Parents' Love

God's magnanimity *with us* is a call *for us* to be magnanimous to others. I have seen God's generous love mirrored in parents who remain faithful to a child who has repeatedly failed and disappointed them, a child who has broken with his family, has become addicted to drugs, has a child out of wedlock, refuses to darken a church door, and is spending time in jail for armed robbery. The district attorney wants to keep him in jail for the rest of his life. Some friends and family members have given up on him and have urged his parents to cut their son loose and not allow him to ruin their lives any longer.

While the parents agree with much of the criticism, they still care for their son. They have hope and remain faithful to their son, remembering the good in him. They'll visit him in jail regularly. They'll continually reach out to disillusioned family members and friends and ask that they forgive him.

Parents who act with such magnanimous love challenge us to be more giving in our love for others. Sometimes our tendency to be logical and reasonable, our "commonsense" approach to caring for people, needs to be set aside. Sometimes we need to suspend all such good judgment and embrace foolishness. We need to stand by a person whom the majority of people consider hopeless. Many would consider the human race hopeless, yet God, the loving Parent, still stands by us, even with our flaws and weaknesses, even when he disapproves of our actions. He is always there.

The Story of Hosea and Gomer

One of my favorite stories from the Bible tells of God's overwhelming love for us through the story of a priest of God named Hosea. He was a good priest. He prayed and made sacrifices in the Temple.

One time when he was in prayer, God spoke to him in a clear way. Hosea couldn't believe what he heard from the Lord. But the strange message was so lucid; he knew he had to follow God's command. God said to him, in no uncertain terms, "Go out and marry a prostitute." Of course Hosea's family and the other priests thought he was delusional. But Hosea knew he had to do this because this is what God wanted. So he went down to the red-light district. He saw a pretty lady. He walked up to her and asked her if she would be his bride.

The lady's name was Gomer. His was a strange request, but she made up her mind quickly. He wasn't too bad looking, and being the wife of a priest might give her back some of the respect she had lost as a prostitute.

"Sure, I'll marry you," she said.

He brought her home and soon she conceived a child. And she gave birth to a beautiful boy. Hosea was so happy.

But then trouble came. Gomer started going out at night. She came home pregnant by another man. Hosea's heart was broken. Feeling shame and wanting to prevent her from causing any more trouble, he built a little prison and put thorns around it to try to keep her from leaving. When she gave birth to the second child it was a girl. Although the child wasn't his, Hosea accepted the mother and child. He forgave the infidelity. He loved Gomer very much.

Can you imagine what happened next? Yes, Gomer left her husband and two children and started living with a former lover. Once again Hosea's heart was torn up. He turned to God in prayer and asked for help. God spoke strange and difficult words: "I want you to come up with a large ransom and pay off Gomer's lover so that you can have her back."

Hosea was obedient. He borrowed the money and went to the house of the lover. He had to beg the man to let him have his wife back. The lover laughed at him, but when he saw the money he agreed. Hosea brought Gomer home. There she gave birth to her third child, whose father was her former lover.

Once again Hosea loved her and the children.

God spoke again to Hosea, revealing to him why he had commanded his servant to do the things he had asked him to do. He said that he had asked Hosea to marry a prostitute and love her. That the pain that Hosea experienced in her unfaithfulness is a sign of the pain that God has experienced when his people have not been faithful to him and have run after foreign gods.

What a punch between the eyes! God is so passionately in love with his people that he is willing to accept them back despite their unfaithfulness. This story contradicts what many of us have ingrained in our psyches about what is right and just. God the Father who speaks to Hosea is the same God the Father of whom Jesus speaks in his parable of the owner of the vineyard. The Father's love is all-encompassing. It's beyond our natural inclinations. Think about what would happen to us if we could accept the enormity of God's love as seen in the parable—and not just accept it, but live it? It would open the door to a life of unbelievable peace, joy, and empowerment.

Being Loved Is the Key to Change

The magnanimously giving face of the Father offers us a value system where love is more powerful than hate; peace more enduring than war; generosity more rewarding than selfishness; and forgiveness more affecting than vengeance. This is not to say that dangerous people don't need to be restrained from harming others, nor is this a call to dismiss armies and police forces. This is a call to shift our focus from the ways of the world to the ways of God and to obey God's commandments, thereby tipping the balance of our actions—and the collective actions of the world—in the direction of love, hope, mercy, and empowerment.

The teaching of the parable can be difficult. That all people regardless of the things they do are equally loved by God. We sympathize with Aunt Hazel. But when we live our lives in a state of love and compassion the way Jesus teaches us in the parable, we will usher in unity and peace . . . and isn't that heaven on earth?

Prayer for Reflection

God, thank you for being generous in your love for me. I honestly can't understand how you can love me so much. Your value system is different from mine. I'm unfaithful and you're faithful to me. I'm stingy and you're generous. I'm proud and you're humble. Help me to embrace you and others in your love. And Lord, when those I love fail me, help me to be magnanimous like you when they ask for pardon, or even if they don't.

QUESTIONS FOR DISCUSSION

1. Is God being unjust to the laborers who worked longer? Explain your feelings about God's decision.
2. Should a marriage continue if one of the partners is unfaithful? If so, why?
3. Is love more powerful than hate? If so, explain why.
4. Do I sometimes need to prove to God my worthiness? Meditate on your response.
5. Should there be limits to a parent's forbearance with a wayward child? Why or why not?

II.

Risking

Matthew 25:14–30

"[The kingdom of heaven] will be as when a man who was going on a journey called in his servants and entrusted his possessions to them. To one he gave five talents; to another, two; to a third, one—to each according to his ability. Then he went away. Immediately the one who received five talents went and traded with them, and made another five. Likewise, the one who received two made another two. But the man who received one went off and dug a hole in the ground and buried his master's money. After a long time the master of those servants came back and settled accounts with them. The one who had received five talents came forward bringing the additional five. He said, 'Master, you gave me five talents. See, I have made five more.' His master said to him, 'Well done, my good and faithful servant. Since you were faithful in small matters, I will give you great responsibilities. Come, share your master's joy.' [Then] the one who had received two talents also came forward and said, 'Master, you gave me two talents. See, I have made two more.' His master said to him, 'Well done, my good and faithful servant. Since you were faithful in small matters, I will give you great responsibilities. Come, share your master's joy.' Then the one who had received the one talent came forward and said, 'Master, I knew you were a

demanding person, harvesting where you did not plant and
gathering where you did not scatter; so out of fear I went
off and buried your talent in the ground. Here it is back.'
His master said to him in reply, 'You wicked, lazy servant!
So you knew that I harvest where I did not plant and gather
where I did not scatter? Should you not then have put my
money in the bank so that I could have got it back with
interest on my return? Now then! Take the talent from him
and give it to the one with ten. For to everyone who has,
more will be given and he will grow rich; but from the one
who has not, even what he has will be taken away. And
throw this useless servant into the darkness outside, where
there will be wailing and grinding of teeth.' "

The Father Wants Us to Risk

The parable says that God the Father is a risktaker. He
gives us all talents. He wants us to make them grow. Growing our talents, however, can be a risky business. We can
exercise our talents and fail. Like a businessman who puts
all his savings into a project he believes in, we can go out
on a limb as we try to grow our talents. We might win. And
then again we might lose our shirt. Still, the Father in the
parable is expecting us to enter into the risk. He wants us
to grow what he has given us. He wants us to enter into the
risk knowing well we could lose it all. What a fascinating

insight into God the Father. He has a face that I find terribly exciting!

There's something in me that wants to be like the "smart" servant who had only the one talent. He sat on it. He went with a sure thing. The other two with their flamboyant use of their talents might have ended up with nothing, and then the one who buried his one talent would have been the hero when the master returned. But no, that's not the Father's pleasure.

I've heard God's call to me: "Use the gifts I have given you. Confront your fears of failure. Confront your insecurities. So what if you look like a fool. So what if you fail. I want you to go out on a limb to get a better view. I want you to laugh at your fears. Write a book and take a chance. Stand in front of a TV camera and tell people how much you love me and watch the criticism. Stop giving a boring homily and risk asking people in the congregation to voice their opinion on what the Gospel means. So what if they ask you a question to which you don't have the answers. Learn to speak Spanish and enter into a rich world of new people. So what if you use the wrong words and instead of telling people you were so nervous that you were perspiring, you say that you wet your pants. Believe in me and my love for you even when some people scorn you for not being realistic. Believe that goodness and love are more powerful than evil and hate. When they start laughing at you, ignoring you, or even pushing you around, hang on. I'm with you. I'm going to bless all those risks you've taken.

You've opened the door to my Kingdom coming more force-
fully into the world. Because you've done this I'm going to
give you even more talents. Thanks for risking."

What does God say to you? It might be "Let go of your
need to work in a prestigious high-paying job. Take the risk
and I will provide for you. Do what makes you happy and
work in education. You will be rich spiritually even if your old
friends laugh when you drive an old car and have to give up
the summer house you used to go to." Or "Some people will
call you crazy for adopting a refugee child or a runaway from a
broken home. 'Those kids are dangerous,' they will say. But I
will be there with you. You will find love and grow your family
and be doing my work, so trust in me and be fearless." I could
go on for pages, but I think you get the idea. The Father rewards those who step out of their comfort zone to do his will,
so just ignore the doubters. Your life will grow bigger.

Jesus Was a Risktaker

When I look at the life of Jesus in the Bible, the word *risk*
easily comes to mind. He was continually taking risks. He
was considered so risky that he got crucified. He took a
chance by challenging the legalism of the religious leaders
of his time. He risked overthrowing deep-seated prejudice
by associating with and even making heroes of the "heretical" Samaritans. He risked shaking up male domination in
his society by including women among his disciples. He

risked including two completely opposite people among his apostles when he chose Matthew, who was a tax collector and in cahoots with the hated Romans, along with Simon, who was a Zealot—a terrorist who was completely opposed to people like Matthew. Such a risky business plan could easily have ended in failure.

And then there were his calls to others to risk. "Peter, come follow me. Leave your livelihood of fishing and come let's wander the hills of Galilee preaching repentance and the Kingdom of God. You say you have a wife, a mother-in-law, and children to worry about? Come on. Take a risk with me. Oh, and as you see me walking on the water, sure, come on. Take a risk. Come walk with me."

I wonder what it must have been like to have Jesus walk up to you and ask you to leave your settled, secure life and come with him as he walked through the hills of Galilee calling people to listen to the "Good News." After he showed his disciples how he healed people—the blind, the crippled, the lepers—and even raised the dead, he turned to his disciples and told them to do what he was doing. And he promised even greater signs. Imagine the way their hearts beat as they risked laying hands on the lepers to heal them. Imagine their fear of what people would say if nothing happened as they prayed over a dead person.

They did risk, though, and over two thousand years later we're still reaping the benefits of their choices. The risk-taking face of the Father shone on them, and we know God's salvation as a result.

The Story as a Meditation

Let's get back to the parable and use a little of the Igna-tian imagination as a way of entering more deeply into the mystery of the story. Imagine yourself as the first servant, the one who has five coins. You give the money to a friend who has come up with a new idea. He calls it a windmill. The invention is made of large wooden blades, secured to a building with an outside rotor so it looks like a giant fan. When the wind hits the blades they turn, which moves an internal grinder over a large round stone, smashing grain into a dusty powder. Using this machine in a windy place is a good way of doing more work with less effort. The idea is completely new. For centuries people have used oxen power in their mills. Many realize that the new invention will save them time and energy. The inventor is able to sell many of the new inventions, and you, the servant, the savvy investor, realize a twofold profit on your investment.

Now imagine yourself as the second servant. You want to make a profit on the two coins you've received so you make an investment in a different company. You take a chance and because of perfect timing (the economy is on an upswing) your investment pays off and you double your investment.

Now imagine yourself as the third servant. You seem to be the most prudent of the three servants. You know the master is a hard man, and, to be perfectly honest, he scares you because he's intimidating. You don't want to take a chance and lose the one coin you've been given, so you do what you think is the smart thing. You take the money to your room, move your bed, and dig a hole in the earthen floor. You bury the coin in the hole and then sit and wait for your master to return.

Now, let's switch out of the roles of the servants and be observers. When we look at the three servants, the first one, with his windmill invention, seems to be the most foolish. He could have lost everything and been laughed at for his harebrained idea. Our second servant could have lost everything too. No investment is a sure thing. Neither of these two servants set aside any of the money they were given for a rainy day. They invested all of it. The third servant, the "prudent" one, could have been the hero of the story. In his boring way, he was the one who didn't risk losing anything. Isn't prudence a virtue? So why is this servant chastised?

The answer can be a bit unnerving. Everything from God is a gift, and he wants us to use his gifts for the benefit of his creation. God wants us to trust in him, and when we take risks for God, we demonstrate faith. What this parable promises is that God will not look the other way when we trust in him. Does that mean we should be reckless in our lives? Certainly, we could take a risk and gamble away our paycheck in Las Vegas, possibly leaving our families homeless and hungry, but that's not what the parable says. If you are obedient to your master, meaning God, then the so-called risks you take aren't risks at all; they are actions in alignment with divine grace.

What Are Your Talents?

All of us have talents. What are yours? Whatever they are, God is calling you to use them and to develop them for the good of his creation. The problem is that the process of growing our talents means we are going to possibly expose ourselves to the risk of criticism and failure. Out of a fear of not doing well and of being laughed at, we can just close in on ourselves and not allow our talents to develop.

Think of the little girl who practices the piano and plays fairly well but who will never play in front of others lest she make a mistake. Such fear is not in line with the image of the risk-taking God who urges us to take a chance by using our talents, even if we fail. He wants us to be at the "cutting edge" of life. He wants us to go through the heart-stopping fear involved in taking risks. He wants us to be exciting!

Another way in which we may take risks is in the way we handle money. Money is important. In our world it is a symbol of security and power. Many of us tend to want to hold on to it for a rainy day. But if we listen to the challenge of Jesus' parable, money is not to be held on to. It should be invested and invested wisely. That's the key. God the Father wants us to take a risk, but he wants us to do so with love in mind. Now, we may make an investment to gain more money, but another motivation might be to invest our money to help others to use their talents more effectively. So we give money to charity to help those who are looking to better themselves. This is an investment in the future of another. You may not see a monetary reward, but helping another person develop his or her talent is a reward in itself.

The Risk of Loving

On a final note, let's talk about the risk associated with loving. Have you ever reached out, offering love to another, only to be rejected? As we all know, because I am sure that it has happened to everyone, it hurts terribly. Think of the pain a teenage boy must suffer when he takes the risk of asking a girl to a dance only to be told condescendingly, "No." Or the pain a wife must experience when a marriage of thirty-three years dissolves because her husband no longer wants to be married. Or the love we have given friends or family only to experience indifference or animosity in return.

When we hear these and other stories of rejected love, we can become overly cautious about opening ourselves up to other people. In turn we may run away from accepting the love of others and cast ourselves off as an island. But this parable is meant to teach us that the Father wants us to risk being involved in loving another. Love, as most of us know, is not easy, but God will support us when we are feeling frail and uncertain. Each time we take a risk, he will be with us, through the storms and through those times when we feel ourselves floating in a sea of troubles. Just as

Jesus finds the lost sheep and puts it on his shoulders to carry it back home or when he grasps Peter and saves him from drowning when he sinks while attempting to walk on water.

God the Father is always there. Jesus is always there. Are you willing to take the risk and believe that with your whole mind and your whole soul?

God's desire for us to take risks in love can be seen in one of Jesus' core teachings, the Beatitudes. In his Sermon on the Mount, Christ speaks of the types of people whom God will console and to whom he will give a special blessing. One of his sayings seems very strange: "Blessed are they who mourn, for they will be comforted" (Matthew 5:4). What does that mean? Is God somehow enjoying our wailing and tears? I think not. To me the meaning is that God wants us to risk loving another so completely and unstintingly that when that person leaves us or dies, we are overcome with sorrow. We have so invested ourselves in the other person that our tears flow copiously when it all ends. God the Father, the risktaker, says that it's better to have loved and lost than never to have loved at all.

Prayer for Reflection

Okay, Father, you delight in challenging me to take risks. There's life, there's newness, there's growth in risk taking. I don't like boring. You're not boring, far from it. Still, don't forget I'm a little ship on your big sea. As I heed your call to risk, I want you to rejoice with me when things go well. But stay close to me in failure and disgrace. I will believe you're with me when my world falls apart. Remember, it was your idea for me to risk in the first place, so please grant me your special blessing and watch over me and all those I love. Give me courage. Give me strength. Give me vision to see you more clearly so I can do your will.

QUESTIONS FOR DISCUSSION

1. Name some of the talents you have received from God, and meditate on how you can use them for the betterment of God's creation.
2. Name one of the biggest risks you've ever taken in your life. Did God provide for you?
3. What are you unwilling to risk? Why?
4. Who are the people you know who have risked making a dream come true? What were the results of their actions?

12.

Proud

Matthew 5:14–16

"You are the light of the world. A city set on a mountain cannot be hidden. Nor do they light a lamp and then put it under a bushel basket; it is set on a lampstand, where it gives light to all in the house. Just so, your light must shine before others, that they may see your good deeds and glorify your heavenly Father."

A Proud Father

When I was in the sixth grade I was already six feet three inches tall. I was a good basketball player at that time. When the season came around, I was consumed by nightly practice and then the Saturday morning games at the gym of St. Francis parish in Louisville, Kentucky. Mom and Dad never missed one of my games.

Recently I was going through some old family photos and I discovered a slip of paper on which Dad had written down a list of the baskets I had made in a game. He did that at *every game*. As we rode home after the final shot, my parents would comment on a good move or two that I had made. I also remember their telling relatives who came to visit us how well I was doing.

Simple actions by my folks, but how they strengthened my self-image! I'm certain that their support and praise gave me the confidence to try new things later in life.

When I read the parable of the lamp, it becomes obvious to me that Jesus is telling us that the Father loves us and is proud of us. Certainly, we are not perfect and we make mistakes—just as I never sank every basket I took—but, regardless, God has a prideful smile on his face. The Father delights in his creation and he knows that inside of each of us is a light that should shine on the world to make it a better place.

Yet sometimes it's hard to see God as the proud Father. Many of us have been conditioned to fear God, to think God is indifferent, or to believe that God is a warlike God out to conquer and destroy. How could God be proud of us?

To comprehend this face of God let's compare his feeling for us to the joy parents experience as they look on their infant for the first time in the delivery room. Imagine how proud a parent is when a child takes his first steps, or eats her vegetables for the first time, or learns how to drive, or graduates from high school.

God is like that, and his light shines brighter when our light shines in unison with his. We are so special in his eyes that without us this moment in the world would not be the same. It would not be complete. Instead of dwelling on the erroneous notion that we are insignificant in a vast world, we need to see that all of us are exceptional in the eyes of God. We confidently pray with the psalmist in the Bible as he prays, "Keep me as the apple of your eye" (Psalm 17:8).

Jesus anticipates our fearful reluctance to accept his Father's love. He ends his parable with the metaphor of hiding your light under a bushel basket. What Jesus is trying to say is "Stop! Don't hide! God gave you life so that you could light a path for others in the name of our Father." With all due respect to Jesus, this can be hard to accept. Before many of us can come close to accepting, to believing in this love, we have got to do some serious work on our self-image. Before we can see ourselves in the light of God's proud gaze on us, we've got to overcome a whole bunch of negative images of ourselves.

Our Battle Against Accepting Love

There's something inside of us, a shadow part of us, that is frequently at war with God and the people who love us. We know the right thing to do, yet we do the opposite. Or we don't act at all. There's a part of us that wants to undermine success when it's right within our grasp. Perhaps this is the sin we've inherited from Adam and Eve.

Think of the various ways we push away people who want to love us. We get too busy with work to accept love.

We don't take time to be alone with a friend. We avoid intimate conversations. We don't give praise and support to those we love. We stress the importance of organization and getting things done. We spend a great deal of time in front of the TV.

This running away from intimate love is perhaps one of the main reasons that there are so many divorces. It's hard to imagine that a couple who have loved each other so much can become antagonistic toward each other and break up. Many times this happens because of a deep-rooted, negative self-image. Sometimes we kill the spirit of the person who loves us by abusive words and actions. We want to destroy the other because we don't want to be loved. We don't want to be found out for who we believe we are inside. Sometimes we resist so much that the lover gives up. All the pushing away becomes too much. How sad!

What is it about intimacy and love that makes us run away from God's love and the love of the people in our lives who reach out to us? One reason is that we're afraid of commitment and involvement. We fear that over time, people will get to know the real us and will reject us. We want to be loved but we're afraid to surrender to the love of God and other people. We are suspicious of love. We don't think others love us for the right reason. If they really knew us they wouldn't love us.

Move away for a moment from this self-reflection. Think of people you know whom you admire and who are forever failing to live up to the greatness you see in them.

It might be a spouse, a child, or a friend. We see all kinds of promise. But, sad to say, they never seem to be able to realize their potential. Often it's a subtle revulsion of self that holds them back. As the Father wants us to remove the bushel basket from our light, we long for the one we love to remove the basket, to shine out with all the brilliance we see in him or her.

How Do We Remove That Bushel Basket?

Given all the negativity that many of us battle, how can we ever remove the bushel basket covering our light? What is the key to being more accepting of the love of others? The solution is to accept the Father's love. In the quiet of our hearts, we need to surrender to God's love: "God, although we're overwhelmed with our sense of being unworthy of you, we accept your love. We receive your forgiveness. We believe that you accept us and are even proud of us. Thank you." It's a simple but monumental declaration; it's a statement that brings with it the peace and security many of us have been looking for all our lives. The Father's love for us should become yeast for our souls that lifts us up to love more intensely the members of our family, our neighbors, our fellow workmates, and members of our church community. The love of the Father is a call for us bring this love to our world. Being aware of his care and support, we never have to be afraid.

Something that has obviously strengthened my faith over the years is reading the Bible and reflecting on God's love for the many people whose stories are told in that sacred book. The Bible is filled with accounts of God seeing greatness in people while the world—and even the person himself—didn't. Take Moses, for instance.

As a child he was raised as a prince in the royal house of Egypt. When he was eighteen he learned that he was adopted. He tried to get back to his Hebrew roots. Once he saw an Egyptian abusing an Israelite. He reached out to protect the man and in the process killed the Egyptian attacker. At that moment, his life as he had known it ended. He became a wanted man and had to escape to a far-off country. We next hear of him when he's seventy years old. He's married with children, trying to live in obscurity as a lowly shepherd. He has developed a severe speech defect. He's unable to speak in public.

This is the person God chooses to lead his people from slavery in Egypt to the Promised Land. What in heaven's name was God thinking? Well, he wasn't thinking as we think. He saw something in Moses that no one else did. God loved the fire of his anger. He loved his humble, open faith, that he could believe in a divine call from a burning bush. He was willing to believe in the seemingly impossible: moving the Hebrews out of Egypt's slavery and into the Promised Land. Impossible! Well, not for Moses when God was right behind him. Yes, Moses was God the Father's kind of person! He was not a natural leader, but he believed, and God empowered him to be more than anyone would have thought possible.

The same God who chose Moses is saying to you and me, "You are the light of the world." May God's encouragement and praise help us to use our talents to give glory to God and help usher in the Kingdom.

Returning God's Prideful Love

When we acknowledge God's love, when we hear him say, "I'm proud of you," we're humbled. We know how unworthy we are of his pride. We know our recurring sins, our fears, our doubts, and our infidelity. We shake our heads in disbelief. But in the face of God's urging we timidly say yes.

After acknowledging and accepting God's prideful love, we naturally want to respond somehow. As God praises us, there's something in us that wants to return the praise. We want to tenderly let God know that we are proud of him.

The Bible gives us the words we need. We relish God's prideful love and return his gift with these words from the Psalms:

PSALM 149

Hallelujah! Sing to the LORD a new song, a hymn in the assembly of the faithful.

*Let Israel be glad in their maker, the people of Zion
  rejoice in their king.*
*Let them praise his name in festive dance, make music
  with tambourine and lyre.*
*For the LORD takes delight in his people, honors the
  poor with victory.*

PSALM 150

*Hallelujah! Praise God in his holy sanctuary; give
  praise in the mighty dome of heaven.*
*Give praise for his mighty deeds, praise him for his great
  majesty.*
*Give praise with blasts upon the horn, praise him with
  harp and lyre.*
*Give praise with tambourines and dance, praise him
  with flutes and strings.*
*Give praise with crashing cymbals, praise him with
  sounding cymbals.*
*Let everything that has breath give praise to the LORD!
  Hallelujah!*

Aside from the Bible, I had a delightful experience of
how to give praise to God for his love. Several years ago, I
hosted the television nun Mother Angelica. Coming to California from Birmingham, Alabama, she wanted to see the
Pacific Ocean. By the time we got to the water, the sun had
gone down. As we moved to a rocky spot along the coast,

the bright moon showed the luminescent crashing waves. Mother stood in silence for a moment and then, with a smile on her face, started applauding and shouting "Hurray, God!" for the wonder of creation.

In our busy world of responsibilities and deadlines, we would do well to imitate Mother Angelica's praise of God. All it takes is a few moments in the day to admire the mountain, the tree, the flower, the breeze, the thunder, or the quiet stare of an infant in her mother's arms. Acknowledge the Father's wonderful work. Say "Hurray" with a big smile. Show how proud you are of Him. Sure, go ahead. Give the Lord a clap!

Expressing My Pride in Others

Enriched by God's pride, we more easily can find ourselves praising and being proud of others. God's love helps us overcome our insecurities. Those insecurities naturally hold us back from praising and expressing our pride in others. "If I tell my wife that I'm proud of her, she'll think I'm weak and I'll lose control and power over her." Only in the security of God's prideful love can we risk praising and expressing our pride in others.

We move from "safe" praise like "That was a nice golf shot," "You did well on that test," and "This meal is delicious" to the more risky praise of "Your love and friendship through the years have given me hope, joy, and meaning.

My world is better for you being in it. Your goodness and faithfulness have allowed me to make my dreams come true. I'm proud of you." Saying this exposes part of our deepest self. We fear rejection. But on the other hand, if we are accepted the rewards are transformative.

The more we surrender to the Father's pride in us, the more we're able to reflect the pride we feel for the people in our lives: spouses, children, brothers and sisters, teachers, coworkers, bosses, and even religious leaders. And that can help us transform the world.

Prayer for Reflection

God, thank you for being proud of me. Help me to accept your love and the love of others. Stand with me as I fight through my negative self-image so that I might see a little of the good you see in me. May your confidence in my goodness enable me to praise you and uplift others.

QUESTIONS FOR DISCUSSION

1. Name a person whose love you have accepted and meditate on how that love has changed your life.
2. Name a person whose love you have rejected. Why did you do so, and what were the consequences of your actions?
3. Meditate on the life of someone with whom you

are frustrated because he or she isn't open to the potential you see in him or her. Is there anything you can do to help this person?

4. Why are many of us fearful of intimacy?

5. Do you believe in the Father's pride in you? Why?

13.

Patient

Matthew 13:24–30

"The kingdom of heaven may be likened to a man who sowed good seed in his field. While everyone was asleep his enemy came and sowed weeds all through the wheat, and then went off. When the crop grew and bore fruit, the weeds appeared as well. The slaves of the householder came to him and said, 'Master, did you not sow good seed in your field? Where have the weeds come from?' He answered, 'An enemy has done this.' His slaves said to him, 'Do you want us to go and pull them up?' He replied, 'No, if you pull up the weeds you might uproot the wheat along with them. Let them grow together until harvest; then at harvest time I will say to the harvesters, "First collect the weeds and tie them in bundles for burning; but gather the wheat into my barn."'"

God the Farmer

God is like a patient farmer. Rather than immediately plucking out and burning the weeds, he waits for harvest time, not wanting to damage the good crop. This is rather comforting. God, the good farmer, knowing that there is great wealth and abundance in all of us, even if part of our life includes things that could be detrimental to our physical, emotional, and spiritual life, wants to support us nonetheless with cultivation, trimming, watering, sunshine, a bit of frost, and of course some fertilizer along the way. Essentially, God does everything possible to help us grow and gives us strength and nourishment so that we can outgrow the weeds around us.

As we move from infancy to adulthood, we encounter a mixture of the good and the bad, the ugly and the beautiful, many times existing side by side with each other. As we grow in all ways, our life becomes a journey of discovery and discernment—and like any journey, it involves process and patience. We develop, we learn, we understand—these are the ways of nature. God has made us this way, and because of that fact he is patient with us as we grow, knowing that there will be times when we succeed, when we stumble, and when we fail.

Part of our growth involves making decisions. Whether we know it or not we are confronted with choices almost every minute of every day. For example, should we say yes or no to an invitation to go out to dinner? Should we hire this person or that person? Should we confront someone we love who has become too involved with church and is neglecting her family? The list is endless. And many times as we journey through life we have to choose between what's right and what's wrong. Often there isn't a clear-cut distinction between the two. At times we move down one road that seems okay only to find we're going the wrong way. We turn around and journey back toward where we came from only to find a maze with many more options. Life can be complicated and confusing. Yet if we have faith in God and we act on that faith, then we know that regardless of where we are *at*, we are moving closer and closer to him. Part of that faith includes banking on God's patience. He knows we're in process. He understands the mistakes that come with growing.

The Patience of God

Few things happen overnight. Life takes time, and we can be sure of God's patience when we watch a rose move from bud to blossom or when we see a newborn baby. Then there is nature: the Grand Canyon; a redwood tree that has been growing for hundreds of years; a mountain that was formed over a million years; a star whose light may take a billion years to traverse the galaxy.

Hurray! What a joy to know that God loves us so much that even in the mystery of our human situation, when we're a mix of saint and sinner, he's patient with us. Oh, what peace comes when we realize in our heart of hearts that God's love is enduring and unwearied!

Having Patience with Myself

Often we have a difficult time being patient with ourselves. So much so that we can beat ourselves up mentally. How often have we said to ourselves, "Why can't I ever get organized? What I need is some discipline. I should have been done with this already"? This kind of thinking can lead to a conditioning in our lives that isn't advantageous for us in our hearts and our souls.

One of my life's lessons on being patient with myself came in my sophomore year in high school in geometry class. I've always struggled with math. Word problems in grade school left me very befuddled. First-year algebra was a bear. I felt I was the worst in the class and holding everyone else up with my questions. Then came geometry. I began the class year with fear and trembling. Our teacher was Father Tom Lavin. He was a firm disciplinarian who could also charm you with his South Side Chicago humor. Whenever I got lost in a lesson (which was quite often), Father Lavin would stop the flow of the class to make sure I understood. I could feel the impatience of my classmates who just wanted to move ahead. But Father Lavin waited until I grasped the point he was making, and in time I got pretty good at geometry. I even developed a delight for this branch of math!

Father Lavin's patience taught me a lesson. It helped me to understand the importance of being more patient with myself. He taught me firsthand about kindness and love. We're created in God's image, and at our best we reflect God to others. The patient face of the Father became clear in Father Lavin, and I have never forgotten it.

Having Patience with Others

Many times we don't have the patience to accept others as they are. We want to change them. We want them to like what we like, have the same dreams we have, drive a car the way we think it should be driven. And in addition to being impatient with strangers and coworkers, our frustration can spill over onto the people we love most, our friends and family.

We must come to admit that love means accepting another person as he is, not demanding that he be who we want him to be. True patience with others comes in seeking to see and understand things from their perspective. We cannot control the world, and we only hurt ourselves and others by trying to do so. What we can do, however, is love the world—God's creation—and pray for the patience and humility to relax and accept the will of the Father.

I came to this understanding of the need for patience and acceptance through my experience with a dear friend. I'm always looking for someone who will pick up on what I'm doing with my television ministry and make sure it continues when I am no longer here. Time and again I've invited people to join me as a cohost, and I've tried to get individuals to begin their own ministry using our studio and fund-raising techniques. For many years I worked with a delightful young woman. Outwardly, she had everything a person would need to be a success on television. She was breathtakingly beautiful, intelligent, warm, and articulate. She had a depth of spirituality that reached right through the camera and touched viewers in a profound way.

I had high expectations of her. I really believed that she could be the one to continue what I had started. But over time as I worked with the young lady, many times I would find myself growing troubled and impatient. Something was missing. I was disappointed, and soon my impatience began to grow like a weed. I began to constantly think, "Why can't she do what I want her to do?"

To be successful in a television ministry a TV host has to have the inclination and the drive to raise funds. If you don't raise money to pay for equipment, crew, editing, and airtime, the whole picture doesn't come together. Fundraising means developing relationships with donors and having the guts to ask, "Will you give me a donation?"

I soon realized that my friend didn't have the proper disposition to make a TV ministry work, and in the process I learned a great lesson. I had expectations that weren't her expectations, and in many ways my expectations were selfishly motivated. I kept focusing on what I wanted from her and not on what was best for her. Realizing this, I have been able to let go of my expectations and just let her be who she was meant to be. It was hard, but her life is not mine to control. I had to learn to be patient as God is patient with us.

I'm happy to say that after we stopped working together,

she met the love of her life, married him, and is now the proud mother of a baby girl. I learned a very profound lesson from my experience with her. It is one that I continue to pray, meditate, and act on today.

Being Free to Choose

God has given us the gift and grace of free will, which means we have the power to decide between right and wrong and to distinguish the thousands of different gray areas that lie in between. God wants us to choose him freely, but because we are given this power to decide we can choose to be seduced by not so good things. To put it bluntly, we have the ability to choose evil. Our freedom includes the possibility that in a given situation we may choose war over peace, selfishness over giving, gluttony over helping people who don't have enough food to eat. And while we may plead ignorance at times, as God's children we have a direct responsibility for the active and passive decisions we make that bring suffering and death.

It's funny how many of us react to what goes on around us. Even though deep down we know that God isn't responsible for the chaos people may have chosen, we become impatient with him. We want him to straighten out the messes we read about in the newspapers or watch on cable news stations. We want him to end what we started. End the killing of people in wars. Bring back the young girl who has been abducted by the sex offender. End poverty. And put a stop to all the violence in our schools. Why doesn't he break into our broken world and bring justice, peace, and goodness?

Believe it or not, God does break into our broken world every moment of every day by continually calling us to choose the better way. Sometimes we don't hear the call, but God is constantly working to bring about change through the inspiration he whispers in our hearts and our ears. God patiently calls us to move in his direction. In the midst of a crazy world, prophets do arise and speak out on injustice and raise people's consciousness; teachers instill a love for others in their students; some journalists expose corruption in politics and in the Church; artists call us to the truth through what they sing, dance, write, paint, and act. And sometimes God breaks into our lives with miracles: an incurable disease is cured, an evil act is thwarted by a good Samaritan, or something simple and powerful like rain will arrive to quench a drought.

Blaming God for the evil we have perpetrated in our freedom is misplaced. God, like the patient farmer in the parable, wants us to heed his insistent call to cultivate the wheat in our lives and reject the weeds.

Letting Go of Unhealthy Self Expectations

One of the keys to practicing patience is for us to clarify our expectations. What would happen if we let go of some unhealthy hopes we have of ourselves? You've dreamed of being a major-league baseball player. You were a star in high school and college. You even made a spot on a minor league Double-A baseball team. But after five years you still haven't gotten that call to the majors. What do you do? The decision is tough—and I'm not advocating giving up on your dreams—but perhaps there are times when you need to listen to what your experiences are telling you. Maybe you should hang up your cleats and move on from that expectation to new hopes in life. Perhaps as a couple you married with the expectation that you would have a large family. But here you are, nine years into the marriage, and you're not able to have children. Perhaps now is the time to change your expectations and look into giving your love to children you adopt.

What if we just lived our lives as best we could and relaxed? What if we stopped wishing we were single again and embraced our family? What if we didn't care about impressing others? What if we stopped mentioning important people we might know or have met so that others will think better of us? What if we believed that God loves us so much that we don't have to do anything to impress him? Could we change our motivations for going to church from routine and fear to love and joy by changing our expectations of what God wants from us? This change of view could open the door to a more loving expression of our religious life. Starting from a firm foundation of peace, we could expand outward, instead of allowing ourselves to be weighed down with the burden of false expectations.

Relaxing

I see a close connection between God the Father being represented as the patient farmer and our need to learn to relax. Any farmer is going to have times of intense work: clearing the fields, plowing, planting, weeding, and then waiting. The patient farmer knows there are times when he has to let God do his work while the farmer just sits back. God shouts at us, "Okay, you did your part. Let me do mine. Relax. The rest will renew your strength for the work at harvest time."

Jesus gives us the concept of patiently relaxing with these words:

"Notice how the flowers grow. They do not toil or spin. But I tell you, not even Solomon in all his splendor was dressed like one of them. If God so clothes the grass in the field that grows today and is thrown into the oven tomorrow, will he not much more provide for you, O you of little faith? As for you, do not seek what you are to eat and what you are to drink, and do not worry anymore. All the nations of the world seek for these things, and your Father knows that you need them."
(Luke 12:27–30)

In our world of ulcers, depression, nervous breakdowns, and anxiety attacks, we need to "let go and let God," as the saying goes. I know it's difficult! Personally speaking, I try to get away from my parish one day a week. I need to find a place of quiet and solitude, and I don't necessarily mean I have to go to the top of a mountain. I spend time just looking at the world around me and trying to find something that brings me peace. I pray. I meditate. I sew. I paint. I read a novel. I ride my motorcycle. I work in the garden. I take a nap. I watch a good movie.

I know that a young couple trying to make ends meet and raising children couldn't afford such a luxury. But, even with the big demands being made on us, we all need to find a little time to do something different, something that doesn't add to our stress but helps to alleviate it. The Father longs for us to live a life devoid of worry and fear. I think many of us, myself included, may be a little afraid to relax because if we slow down in our busy life, we might have the opportunity to hear God calling us to service or calling us to fulfill a dream that has been stirring in our hearts for years. That dream may be a far cry from what we're doing now. Maybe a mother of six will write a book, or a construction worker will take up ballet, or a urologist will start to paint, or a corporate executive will go to Mexico to study Spanish. Regardless of the particulars, what God wants us to do is to trust in him and relax in his love.

God's call to patience reminds me of the French poet Charles Péguy. For him, God was a fearsome, judgmental, impatient God who didn't allow him rest. Yet he felt a still quiet voice within him that said that this wasn't the correct picture. In response, Péguy confronted his personal driving restlessness in poems that depicted God in a different light, as a gentle, patient grandfather, sitting on a porch, rocking in his chair and sharing his tender love. Plagued with insomnia, Péguy wrote the poem "Sleep":

> *"I don't like the man who doesn't sleep," says God.*
> *"Sleep is a friend of man.*
> *Sleep is a friend of God.*
> *Sleep is perhaps the most beautiful thing I have*
>   *created.*
> *And I myself rested on the seventh day."*

Isn't that a beautiful poem? We can close our eyes and vividly picture the Father holding us in his arms and caressing us to calm our racing hearts. We can look up at his face, his beautiful face, and we can rest our heads on his breast.

What About Those Weeds

As a final note, let's return to the parable and talk a little about the weeds. In the parable the enemy has planted weeds that will compete with the wheat crop for soil and water and nutrients. The weeds do not provide sustenance for us, but they can choke the plants we're growing to put food on the table. William Barcley says that the weeds that grow along with the wheat in the Holy Land are initially very difficult to identify. Only with time can the weeds be distinguished from the wheat. The farmer is wise to wait patiently until the harvest to separate them.

If we see the farmer as the face of the patient Father, we must face the fact that if we are the Lord's wheat, then we must learn to live with the evil influences of the weeds in our lives. We've got to believe and trust that he's also going to provide us with the strength to resist evil and temptation. Our patient Father cultivates us with lessons from the Bible. We have teachings and commandments that show us how to better discern the weeds from the wheat in our life. Jesus is the most concrete of examples, teaching us to choose what is best for us. His teachings about poverty, mercy, peace, purity of heart, and love help to open our eyes to how to live life to the fullest. God will nourish us in such a way that we can outgrow and vanquish the enemy. He'll give us the warmth, moisture, and stimulation we need to grow to maturity and to be fit for the harvest.

Prayer for Reflection

God, thank you for being patient with me. As I grow I can mess things up so easily. I want to be true to you. Along with calling me to account, hang in with me. You know there are all kinds of evil, both in my heart and coming to me from outside. Help me to be patient with others. Help me to be patient with you. Help me to be patient with myself.

QUESTIONS FOR DISCUSSION

1. What are the weeds that are growing in your life?
2. What person do you wish would change? Why do you feel this need?
3. What makes you most impatient? What steps can you take to endure these situations?
4. What are some of the things you can do to relax?

14.

Trusting

Mark 12:1–9

He began to speak to them in parables. "A man planted
a vineyard, put a hedge around it, dug a wine press, and
built a tower. Then he leased it to tenant farmers and left
on a journey. At the proper time he sent a servant to the
tenants to obtain from them some of the produce of the
vineyard. But they seized him, beat him, and sent him away
empty-handed. Again he sent them another servant. And
that one they beat over the head and treated shamefully.
He sent yet another, whom they killed. So, too, many
others; some they beat, others they killed. He had one
other to send, a beloved son. He sent him to them last of
all, thinking, 'They will respect my son.' But those tenants
said to one another, 'This is the heir. Come, let us kill him,
and the inheritance will be ours.' So they seized him and
killed him, and threw him out of the vineyard. What (then)
will the owner of the vineyard do? He will come, put the
tenants to death, and give the vineyard to others."

The Foolish Farmer

Again, Jesus gives us the image of God as a farmer. Only this time, on the surface, this farmer doesn't seem to be as savvy as our wheat farmer. This grape farmer is a bit of a fool, isn't he? You'd think he would learn. There's no denying he has a right to his share of the grapes. He had made an agreement with the tenants. They would work the land and in exchange for the use of the land, at harvest time they would share the harvest with him.

But the tenants felt entitled to the entire harvest. We can imagine ourselves in their shoes. They had done all the work for almost a year. They had mended the poles on which the grapes would grow and attached the shoots in early fall. They had pulled weeds all through the summer. Then when the air was bitter cold they had begun the harvest. The skin on their necks was a leathery tan. Their hands were callused. They had given all their time to make the harvest possible.

We can also imagine that when the servant of the farmer arrived with a wagon to take away the farmer's share, the tenants were a little angry. They had worked all day harvesting. They wanted to rest. They were tired. Perhaps the owner's servant ticked off the tenants by demanding that they load the grapes onto his wagon. They told the servant to load the grapes himself. He told them that loading wasn't his job. He then called them lazy good-for-nothings.

A fight ensued, further galvanizing in the hearts of the

tenants the belief that they had a right to all the grapes. They demonized the farmer, further justifying their unwillingness to give up any of their grapes.

Meanwhile the farmer couldn't understand the tenants' unwillingness to surrender the grapes. He sent another servant. This one was beaten more severely than the first. He was sent packing. The third servant never returned. The tenants killed him.

Being a highly reasonable and peace-loving man, the farmer kept hoping that he would get the grapes he was owed. He decided to send his son, who shared his father's love and trust. The farmer thought, "Surely, when they see my son coming, the tenants will relent and share the grapes that are rightfully mine."

When the tenants saw the son coming, their sense of justice and what was right had already been perverted by their greed and violence. They thought, "Since this is the farmer's only son, if we kill him the farmer will have no other heirs." In their twisted reasoning they concluded that they would then have a legal claim to the land. When the son approached, they summarily killed him on the spot and threw his body outside the vineyard.

The Father Is Incredibly Persistent

In this story Jesus reveals something about his Father but in a rather unsavory context. There are the nasty tenants who are filled with greed, envy, hatred, and violence. They're thugs who beat up some and kill others. On the other hand, the farmer is a good man, trusting, patient, and not willing to believe in the tenants' persistent evil. He keeps trusting that they will accept the next servant he sends.

Finally the farmer is so convinced that the tenants will change, he risks sending his only son, his most precious treasure, believing they will come to their senses and hand over his share of the grapes.

Jesus is saying to us, "Look at the love of my Father. Time and again he has reached out to you with his servants, the prophets. Their message has been simple: 'Give yourselves to the Father by following his commandments. Love the Father with all your mind, heart, and soul. And love your neighbor as yourself.' The call was clear and simple. You responded by persecuting and killing the prophets. The Father continued to have faith in you, believing that you would change. He finally sent me, his only son." And we know what happened to God's only Son.

The face of the Father Jesus shows us in this parable is that of a persistently trusting person. God's trusting goes to limits that for all practical purposes seem reckless and foolish. Most of us shake our heads in disbelief. We believe we would know where to draw the line; we would never trust in the goodness of others to this extent, not after seeing what had happened so many times before. Imagine someone who is in a situation similar to that of the farmer asking us for advice about what to do. How would we respond? "Stop being a fool. Don't trust them anymore." And we would proudly pat ourselves on the back convinced that we'd given loving counsel. Why should a person continue to sacrifice people he loved to evildoers? And as for the evil people who had committed violence against his servants, we'd demand that they be punished and sent to jail. Wouldn't that be fitting punishment for those bad people?

The farmer's actions seem totally unreasonable to us, yet what Jesus is trying to do is show us that the Father is beyond what seems right and just in our concrete world. God's trust in the goodness of his creation goes beyond any limited vision we have of what is right or wrong.

Dealing with the Trusting Father

Now we must learn to invite this trusting Father to be part of our lives. How do we do this? First we must *accept the reality of this Father's love* by emulating his actions and surrendering to the overpowering confidence we have been shown in the parable. If God can trust in our goodness so much, we can in turn learn to trust in the goodness of God. This can be done with a quiet "yes" that rises out of our soul, an affirmation that there is nothing to fear when we are working with God. Maybe we can shout it in the words of the Creed at our next day of public worship.

Then we've got to *sustain the commitment* with prayer, reading the Bible, and accepting the risk involved in sharing our faith in a trusting God. We can do this by leading through example, by performing good, loving acts that improve the quality of life for family members, neighbors, and people at work or school. We can strengthen the lives of other church members by being people of strong faith, and we can use that power to teach young people and adults alike.

When we accept the trusting love of the Father and don't reject it like the evil tenants, we gain a sense of security that enables us to risk using our talents. We trust ourselves more because we know that God has our back. With the Father's trust and our commitment to him, we find a new strength to empower the people around us. Because of God's trust we more easily can risk saying to another, "I love you." We can accept the burden of a relationship with another and embrace responsibility. We can realize a dream and go back to school to start a new direction in our life.

Who Are Today's Prophets?

As signs of his trust, God has repeatedly sent servants to remind people that the bounty of life comes from God. This brings to mind the prophets God sent to his people, those who call us back to his love and the love of others. In our technologically advanced world, with so many people talking and vying for attention, how do we recognize the new prophets? Who are today's Amos, Isaiah, Ezekiel, Daniel, Elijah, and Jeremiah? Who are today's prophets who call us to God and to justice for others? I think of men and women who give up lives of comfort to serve the millions of refugees who suffer the injustice of war. Often these people are abused, imprisoned, and killed. I think of the Civil Rights leaders who faced down the Ku Klux Klan and corrupt forces of Jim Crow during the 1950s and 1960s; the brave activists who face down drug cartels and human smugglers to assist immigrants on our southern border; and people like Sister Dorothy Stang, who was murdered in Brazil in 2005 for defending the rights of indigenous people from loggers seeking to clear-cut the Amazon rain forest. There are people who stand up to injustices committed against women, the sick, children, and the elderly. They are persecuted and often suffer a death that takes the form of rejection and scorn.

These prophets have heard a call from suffering people and have been willing to accept the all-too-real possibility that in lending a hand they could face intense suffering and death. They are urged on by the Father's trusting love to give of themselves to preach the Good News of God's trusting love for all. Many of these people remain nameless; they are never featured on a TV show or on a news program, but they are out there. God continues to send prophets in unlikely guises. Sometimes the person behind an opera, a ballet, a sculpture, a movie, or even a pounding piece of rap music can be a prophet. These prophets too can suffer pain and rejection, facing mockery or death threats when their message challenges the status quo.

The parable shows us that the servants were not accepted. Most people, even purported religious people, are not comfortable with prophets. Prophets are thorns in our sides; they force us to look at ourselves and the world around us. Many of us put up a wall and become insensitive to them and their message. We don't want to give up our way of acting. We make excuses for not serving others: Let someone else more qualified take care of the poor; I just don't have the temperament to make a change; I'm too young and no one will listen to me; I'm too old and feeble to serve in any way. All these excuses. We are called and what do we do?

Nothing.

How to Respond to a Prophet

Jesus gives us a lesson in how to respond to the call of a prophet. John the Baptist was Jesus' prophet. When he was around thirty years old Jesus heard that John was preaching. He did the first thing required in responding to a prophet—he *moved*. He took action. He went from Nazareth to a spot near where the Jordan River flows into the Dead Sea. The trip is about ninety miles. If we want to listen to God's messengers we have to act, to move out of our comfort zone, to move away from where we live and go someplace new. The move might be down the street or across the country or even across the sea.

Next Jesus humbly entered the water and was baptized by the prophet John. After we take action, after we move, we need to *express our surrender* to the prophet's call to give our life to God. In the Catholic Church we do that through participation in the sacraments. Being baptized, walking down the aisle to receive Communion, and committing ourselves in marriage are expressions of surrender. I surrendered when the bishop laid his hands on my head at my ordination. Another might respond to an altar call at a revival. Another might tell her story of faith at a small prayer meeting.

When Jesus came out of the water the Bible says that the Holy Spirit called him into *the desert*, where he prayed and fasted for forty days. This time of discernment after a public commitment is vital before embarking on a strong ministry. Paul tells us that after his encounter with Jesus on the road to Damascus he spent three years in the deserts of Arabia. Men and women who desire to enter into a religious community are required to go through a desert experience called the novitiate, which involves one or two years of isolation, prayer, and meditation. During my two years in the novitiate I experienced the long retreat. This is thirty days of strict silence. During that time I had to come face-to-face with my temptations and my insecurities. Was I doing all this for the right reasons? How could I help those around me? This time of turning their gaze toward God and asking for guidance in fulfilling their mission, their vocation, is vital for giving friars, nuns, and monks a clear vision of the work they are to do.

The final response of Jesus to the call of the prophet was

to share the love of the Father with others. The same call Jesus responded to continues today. As the parable shows, God gives us freedom but trusts that we will answer.

Jesus' way to respond to the call of the prophet is to move, to express surrender, to go to the desert, and then courageously to share the love of God.

The Father Is Trusting but Not a Pushover

Finally, there is another aspect of the Father's face that comes through in this parable. After the son is murdered, the farmer ends his trusting and kills the wretched tenants. The message: God is patient, God is trusting, but don't take God for granted. Sending his Son was his final message. Accept the Son, don't crucify him with your actions, with your deceit, with your anger. God the Father trusts in our goodness, but if we are erring, we are called to change. Why wait? Now is the best time to start.

Prayer for Reflection

> *God, thank you for being so unbelievably trusting of me despite my sins. How many times have I failed to live up to the dream you have placed in my heart. Open my eyes to the prophets you send into my life. Help me to imitate Jesus' response to the call of John the Baptist. And Lord, don't let me cheapen your trust in me by not accepting the change you expect of me right now.*

QUESTIONS FOR DISCUSSION

1. Call to mind some people in your life who are trusting. How do they relate to others? What can you learn from them?

2. If you were the farmer, how would you have reacted to the rebuff of the first servant you sent? Why?

3. In your eyes and heart, who are today's prophets and what can you learn from them?

4. Discuss the importance of a desert experience. Have you had one?

15.

Optimistic

Matthew 13:3

"A sower went out to sow. And as he sowed, some seed fell on the path, and the birds came and they ate it up. Other fell on rocky ground, where it had little soil. It sprang up at once because the soil was not deep, and when the sun rose it was scorched, and it withered for lack of roots. Some seed fell among thorns, and the thorns grew up and choked it. But some seed fell on rich soil, and produced fruit, a hundred or sixty or thirtyfold. Whoever has ears ought to hear."

Encouragement for Disciples

Throughout Jesus' ministry his motley crew of disciples was running into walls of failure. Although Jesus had empowered them to continue his work of preaching, healing, driving out Satan, and working wonders of nature, they were discouraged by their lack of success.

Many of those who initially accepted the Good News

didn't follow Jesus for long. Many of these people eventually turned away from the message that the disciples were proclaiming. Some were overcome by fear, some gave up when trouble and persecution came, and some fell away by seduction of the world's pleasures and wealth. The majority could have cared less about attending to what the disciples said or did.

Jesus used this parable to bolster the spirits of his disciples as well as those of us who follow God. In the midst of their lack of success he wanted to assure the faithful that the face of the Father is optimistic, that their work wasn't in vain. By using an example they were all familiar with—planting seeds—Jesus helped his disciples to see that proclaiming the word of God, though difficult and at times disconcerting, could be fruitful nonetheless.

All around them farmers could be seen sowing seeds in their fields. In Jesus' time farmers didn't have the convenience of machines that would plant seeds. A sower would wait for a good rain. Then he would cultivate his field by hand or using a beast of burden. Stowing the seeds in the fold of his garment, he would take the seeds by the handful and throw them out over the field. Some seeds worked. The majority failed.

Jesus' Failures

The disciples could also take consolation from the many failures Jesus experienced. Even though Jesus was the Son of God, and the Son of God could do anything, he seems to have failed on numerous occasions. He spoke to masses of people, and many of them ignored his message of faith, hope, and love. When he spoke to his hometown people, those who knew him well in Nazareth, they turned on him and wanted to kill him:

> *They rose up, drove him out of the town, and led him*
> *to the brow of the hill on which their town had been*
> *built, to hurl him down headlong. (Luke 4:29)*

Mark tells us that even Jesus' family wanted to take him away from his ministry because they thought he was insane:

> *Again [the] crowd gathered, making it impossible for*
> *them even to eat. When his relatives heard of this they*
> *set out to seize him, for they said, "He is out of his*
> *mind." (Mark 3:20–21)*

Later, the crowds of people misunderstood the purpose of his miracles and preaching and wanted to raise him up as a king to overthrow the Romans, missing the point completely that his "Kingdom" was not one of land and borders:

> *When the people saw the sign he had done, they said,*
> *"This is truly the Prophet, the one who is to come into*
> *the world." Since Jesus knew that they were going to*

come and carry him off to make him king, he withdrew
again to the mountain alone. (John 6:14–15)

It seems that Jesus gave up preaching to them directly
and spoke mostly in parables because, as he explained to
his disciples:

"'[T]hey look but do not see and hear but do not listen
or understand.' Isaiah's prophecy is fulfilled in them,
which says: 'You shall indeed hear but not understand,
you shall indeed look but never see. Gross is the heart
of this people, they will hardly hear with their ears,
they have closed their eyes, lest they see with their eyes
and hear with their ears and understand with their
heart and be converted, and I heal them.'" (Matthew
13:13–15)

Even the religious leaders, those dedicated to the Father, wanted to kill him. "I know that you are descendants
of Abraham. But you are trying to kill me, because my word
has no room among you" (John 8:37). Peter, one of his most
intimate friends, denied him three times. Judas, one of his
inner circle, betrayed him to the authorities who ultimately
had him killed. Even on the cross, Christ felt so alone that
he "cried out in a loud voice, *'Eloi, Eloi, lema sabachthani?'*
which is translated, 'My God, my God, why have you for-
saken me?'" (Mark 15:34).

Although this cry of despair came from the depth of

his suffering body, he was able to reach out in confident love and surrender to his Father, with whom he was one, and say with his final breath, "Into your hands I commend my spirit."

I like to imagine that if Jesus were trying to convince his disciples of the fruitfulness of their ministry today in the midst of failure, he'd talk about baseball. A baseball player who strikes out seven out of ten times at bat—that means he fails 70 percent of the time—is such a valuable asset to the team that he can garner a multimillion-dollar salary. His picture will be featured on cereal boxes and crowds of people will seek his autograph. If he fails seventy times and succeeds thirty times he's a star! Failures happen, but that is no reason to be discouraged. At the end of the day, we have to look at the big picture and realize that in the midst of defeat we can still be victorious.

Resurrection Victory

For us followers of Jesus, the victory of his Resurrection is the key to our overcoming failure with success. From the seeming defeat of Good Friday, we move to the triumph of the Resurrection—to a place in our hearts where we can live the confidence of life's victory over death. Through the good news of this miracle, each of us can reflect on experiences of failure in our lives with the eyes of faith. And if we listen carefully we can hear the optimistic words of the Father; we can see the fruit that comes out of failure.

I'd like to share a story with you, one that pains me a bit, but I hope it will illustrate a point. Many years ago I was teaching high school immediately after my ordination to the priesthood. Despite my lofty aspiration to teach in a high school in the riot-torn district of Watts in Los Angeles, it just didn't work out. I had to give up teaching after two years. I felt I was a complete failure. I wasn't able to maintain discipline. My classes were disasters of unruly and loud chaos. I resigned with great disgrace and humiliation. I felt despondent. I had failed right at the start of my life as a priest, and I thought nothing good would ever come out of that experience. Only years later did I realize the value of that difficult time. My failure became my strength in some ways because it enabled me to relate and bring healing to many people who had experienced monumental disappointments in their marriages, in raising their children, in their jobs, and in ill health. Many of these people felt that life had lost all meaning, just as I had felt in those very trying years. But the depth of my own failure helped me connect with others and to raise many of those failures to victory through the power of the Resurrection.

The Parable's Call to Preach— Where and How

The parable reminds us that we are called to share with others the seeds of the Good News we have received. We are called to join the disciples as they go out into the world preaching, healing, casting out Satan, and working wonders. Lest we be discouraged, the Father assures us that our efforts will return a rich, rich harvest. All we have to do is risk sowing the seeds.

Practically speaking, how do we do that? There are various ways of responding to the parable's challenge. We might preach in churches, street corners, around the dining room table, in classrooms, on football fields, next to a hospital bed, and on YouTube. Some of us may be called more dramatically. We might pursue a life as a missionary who travels to foreign lands and enters into different cultures and speaks different languages.

We can share the Good News with a lot of head knowledge. We can quote the Bible chapter and verse. We can call on the authority of learned scholars or known spiritual leaders. We can also simply speak about our personal encounter with God with eloquence or simplicity. We can preach without saying a word by handing a sandwich to a homeless person living under a bridge or setting the bone of an injured child in a hospital.

The parable reminds us that we are to give to others the blessings we have received. Our orientation should not be to selfishly keep our encounters with God to ourselves. With joyful giving we should try to share what we have received.

Preparation for Sharing the Good News

To share the Good News we need to make some prepara-
tion. First we need to admit that *the Father is the driving
power* behind our desires to evangelize. The Father is our
creator and sustainer. He has sent his son to call us to himself. We humbly respond to his call to bring the Good News
to others. We turn to God for help in prayer. We need to
come to God each morning and ask for his encouragement
and direction. This time can involve formal prayer or quiet
meditation. Our prayers can be as brief as a few seconds.
God will walk with us today as we share his love.

As we move out into the field to do the will of God, we
need to keep our eyes and ears open at all times. Certainly,
life will happen, and we will be faced with the day-to-day
tasks of getting out of bed, eating breakfast, and going to
work, but let's watch out for the *surprises*: the phone call
from an old friend, the lady we see trying to herd three
unruly children at the grocery store, the loud man at the
table next to yours in the restaurant, or the coworker who
has become suddenly quiet. A good evangelist believes that
God is going to put into your life the people to whom you
are supposed to bring the Good News. Be ready and be
aware. This is true optimism.

And always be willing to *listen*. It's always better to listen before you speak. Real Christian listening means you
are trying to love the person you're with and to respect
what he or she has to say, to give up your own ego so your

own thoughts aren't getting in the way of the words that are being said to you. When we meet the people in our lives we need to listen with love. We need to look and study their physical aspects: the color and movement of their eyes, the tone of their skin, the cut of their hair, their posture, their hand movements, the way they walk, and their clothes. Pick up on their spirit: fears, joys, sadness, courage, foolishness, doubt, anger, indifference. Pick up on what they like or dislike. Learn about their family. How did they meet their marriage partner? What are their fears and dreams? Try to know them more deeply. Only with knowing and loving a person can we be able to find the fertile ground to lay the seeds of God's love. We find this love together, in relationships.

That listening, knowing, and loving might take a long time: days, months, years. Or it may happen quickly. No matter what, the parable says that we've got to be sharers with others of the Good News. And the better we know and love others, the more likely that the power of God's love will take root in them and they will become living examples of Jesus' life here on earth.

Who Are the Members of the Hundredfold Success?

But that still leaves a lot of questions about who is in that "successful" category of the "hundred or sixty or thirtyfold." How do we identify them? What do they say and do? If they believe in God, is that enough? Do they believe in Jesus? Do they belong to a certain denomination or religion? Are they baptized? Do they go to church regularly or periodically, or only for funerals and weddings? Do they read the Bible? Do they pray? And what about their relationships with others? Do they love those around them by doing service? Are they meeting Jesus, as in the parable of Matthew 25:31–46, giving a drink to the thirsty, food to the hungry, clothes to the naked? Welcoming strangers, visiting the sick and imprisoned? Is that enough? Even if they don't profess faith in organized religion, can they get into heaven? Is Jesus offering salvation to the at least one billion people on the earth today who will never even hear his name mentioned?

And what about the words of John in his first letter? "Everyone who loves is begotten by God and knows God" (1 John 4:7). Is the way to God through my loving my marriage partner and children? Is that going to be the final question God asks me when I'm judged at my death? Is all that churchgoing secondary to loving the people in my life? Is the criterion for success those who make it to heaven?

To be honest, I agree that these are all important questions, vitally important questions. I have to admit that I don't have the answers. And that's okay. I'm glad I don't have to be overly concerned with the answers to these questions. As I study the faces of God in the parables, I'm in awe at how little I know of God. When faced with these sensitive and vital questions, I need to let God be in control. From what I've gathered from the parables, God's love is overpowering.

In the midst of these questions about who are the successes in God's eyes, I can rest secure that God loves every person he's created more than I can ever imagine.

Letting Go of Judgments

Practically speaking, we need to stop being so judgmental. "Stop judging and you will not be judged. Stop condemning and you will not be condemned" (Luke 6:37). We need to let go of spending time worrying about and judging others and make sure that we are working with God on making ourselves better people. Each person needs to concentrate on being the best Jew, Muslim, Christian, or even unbeliever he or she can be. There is surrender to the belief that God, the Creator and Sustainer of creation and all people, fervently loves all creation and all people. God is doing all in his power to call everyone to himself with more persuasiveness than we could ever imagine. We see this love for all when Jesus breaks out of the confines of his people's expectations of whom to associate with and whom to love. He went to Samaritans and Gentiles. As a priest I recite the words of Consecration over the wine during Mass, taken from the Gospel of Mark: "This is my blood of the covenant, which shall be shed for many" (Mark 14:24).

That doesn't mean that we say that one religion or denomination is as good as the other. No, but it does mean embracing our beliefs wholeheartedly while respecting the convictions of others. We need to be convinced that we are doing the correct thing with our lives. We are continually strengthening our faith through listening to the teachings and faith of our community and living these lessons. We pray and read the Bible in the spirit of our tradition. Moreover we are called to share our beliefs with others through our words but most importantly through our actions.

Now, judging is a natural and necessary part of life. We make judgment calls all the time, from commenting on a person's outfit to deciding whether we should marry a certain person, to deliberating on a jury. But I believe that when Jesus told us not to judge, he was talking about not judging where people stand in their relation with God. Judge not and you will not be judged. Rather than wasting time, we are called to put away our condemnations of others and concentrate on discovering the good in them. This is a way of thinking more and more like God. Rather than judge people of other religions, we are called to seek ways in which God is manifesting himself in them. This way of seeing humbly will ultimately make us better people, and when we are better people we can serve God more effectively.

We are missionaries of the Father, and our job is to love all creation, to live in faith, and to seek God in the lives of all people. When we are asked about our faith we respond with humble confidence. Our ultimate goal is being one with the Father, and when that happens we become one with all his creation.

Hear the parable's call to share the Good News of the Father's love. There is forgiveness and salvation for everyone if they want it. Don't be overwhelmed by indifference or antagonism. Optimism is a form of faith, and when we think of the lovely face of God, the ultimate optimist, we can be certain that the Lord is in our life right now and is going to use our efforts to call countless people to himself.

Prayer for Reflection

God, stand by me when I try to share with others the love you have shown me. You know that I'm easily discouraged. Lift me up. Help me to look fully at your face and see your love for me in your eyes. I'm amazed that you want to work with me and blessed with this life you've given me. Help me to live up to your expectations of greatness. Thank you for believing in me.

QUESTIONS FOR DISCUSSION

1. How do you react to Jesus' failures?
2. Recall a significant failure in your life. What has been its value?
3. Imagine you are speaking to an unbeliever. How would you explain your faith to that person?
4. Are you reluctant to share your faith? Why?
5. Who seems to be the best evangelist for God today?
6. Who do you think are the members of the hundredfold of the parable?

Conclusion

Our relationship with God is a never ending journey. We are learning new things about God all the time, and in the process we are learning new things about ourselves as well. My challenge to create television programs based on the parables of Jesus evolved into this book, and I feel blessed to have had so many encounters that helped reveal to me the many faces of the Lord. Through many hours of praying, talking, searching Scripture, writing and rewriting this book, I feel like I've grown closer to God in a way I never expected, and I hope that your journey with me through this book has a similar effect.

So the journey continues. As we reach out to God, we are blessed with a rich return of love from the Father. This happens through his creation. Always be on the lookout because we are being called to turn our face toward God's face whenever we encounter the glory of a mountain, a tail-wagging greeting by a dog, a funny movie, a stranger's smile, the sad news of the death of a friend, a reading from the Bible, a touching song during Mass, a person of a different religion lifting his voice in praise of God. It is through these encounters, and not just these, but through all encounters that God reveals his many beautiful faces.

I think of the many faces I wear in my life: I try to evoke a smile from a one-year-old by twisting my face in a clownish way. I speak words of comfort to a widow during a funeral with a somber but hopeful look. My eyes squint, my mouth opens, I gasp for air, and I break into a cacophonous laugh after hearing a good joke. My face turns red with embarrassment when I don't have a clue how to answer a simple question. And I let all those muscles in my face relax when I put my head on the pillow at night and surrender to sleep.

So many sides to me. So many sides to you. So many sides to God. All of us are a rich blend of many faces, and we are wonderful mysteries to be constantly explored.

I do hope that this little quest through some of the faces of the Father presented by Jesus in these fifteen parables has opened up for you the thrilling hunger to look into the eyes of God and all creation and say, I love you.

Parables

Lost sheep (Luke 15:4–7)

Lost money (Luke 15:8–10)

The prodigal son (Luke 15:11–32)

Hidden treasure (Matthew 13:44)

Pearl of great price (Matthew 13:45–46)

Unfruitful fig tree (Luke 13:6–9)

Obedient and disobedient sons (Matthew 21:28–32)

Wicked tenants (Matthew 21:33–46)

Patching the old cloak (Matthew 9:16)

Putting new wine into a new wine skin (Matthew 9:17)

Sower and the seed (Matthew 13:3–8)

Weeds among the wheat (Matthew 13:24–30)

Mustard seed (Matthew 13:31–32)

Yeast (Matthew 13:33)

Net (Matthew 13:47–50)

Great dinner (Luke 14:16–24)

The seed growing secretly (Mark 4:26–29)

House built on rock (Matthew 7:24–27)

Pharisee and tax collector (Luke 18:9–14)

The sinful women and two debtors (Luke 7:36–50)

Wedding feast of the king's son (Matthew 22:1–14)

Lamp under a bushel basket (Matthew 5:15–16)

Unforgiving servant (Matthew 18:23–35)

Friend at midnight (Luke 11:5–13)

Persistent widow (Luke 18:1–8)

Planning a tower (Luke 14:28–30)

King with 10,000 troops against 20,000 troops (Luke 14:31–33)

Good Samaritan (Luke 10:30–37)

Dishonest steward (Luke 16:1–13)

Workers in the vineyard (Matthew 20:1–16)

Ten virgins with lamps (Matthew 25:1–13)

Three servants get talents (Matthew 25:14–30)

Ten gold coins to ten servants (Luke 19:12–27)

Sheep and goats (Matthew 25:31–46)

Master expects servants to do duty (Luke 17:7–10)

Watchful servants rewarded (Mark 13:34–37; Luke 12:36–48)

Rich fool builds barns (Luke 12:16–21)

Rich man and Lazarus (Luke 16:19–31)

"You are the salt of the earth" (Matthew 5:13; Luke 14:34–35)

Let your light shine (Matthew 5:15–16)

Acknowledgments

Special thanks to my cousin Nan Kotowski for her loving and wise direction in the formation of the book. Pat Connor, SVD, gave his grammatical and theological insights. Joerg Wellbrink offered his family-oriented direction all the way from Germany. Louise and Frank McDonald opened the door to their Lake Gregory home to allow me to escape to write.

The team of people responsible for our weekly TV program at Wordnet Productions has patiently borne with my time away from the studio as I wrote and rewrote the manuscript.

My religious community, the Society of the Divine Word, has given me love, support, and encouragement.

The publishing of the book happened only through the expert persuasion of my agent, Loretta Barrett.

Maggie Carr did a masterful job of copyediting.

Finally, thanks to Gary Jansen, the religion editor of Doubleday. The challenges of his insights into good writing and spirituality have prodded me to strive for excellence.

Father Michael Manning, a member of the Society of the Divine Word, is a Catholic priest who has served as a high school teacher, vocation director, provincial, prison chaplain, and pastor. He is a popular speaker at parish missions, conventions, and international retreats.

His main work has been hosting an internationally syndicated television program each week. His goal is to present Catholic perspectives from the Bible with a special emphasis on building bridges among denominations and religions.

With Wordnet Productions he produces forty programs a year. They air on the Trinity Broadcasting Network, several Catholic diocesan cable networks, and the U.S. Armed Services network, which sends the program to every U.S. military base and ship at sea around the world. His programs can be viewed 24/7 on his web page www.wordnet.tv.

He has appeared on *Larry King Live*, the *Nancy Grace* program, Robert Schuler's *Hour of Power*, and *The Tonight Show with Jay Leno*.

His previous books include *Pardon My Lenten Smile*, *Proclaimed from the Rooftops*, *A Life Full of Surprises*, *On Camera and Off* (an autobiography), *Questions and Answers for Today's Catholics*, and 5 *Seconds a Day to a Successful Marriage*. He also wrote *Paul*— a musical on the life of Saint Paul.

Father has degrees in philosophy and theology and a master of fine arts in playwriting.

His religious community, the Society of the Divine Word, serves the poor with the Good News in over seventy countries.

Father Mike lives in San Bernardino, California.

Contact him:
www.wordnet.tv (watch his programs online)
mail@wordnet.tv
www.youtube.com/mikesvd